ADARReview

Foreign Service Officer Test
2013 Edition

Complete Guide to the
Written Exam and Oral Assessment

LIMIT OF LIABILITY/DISCLAIMER OF WARRANTY: THE PUBLISHER AND THE AUTHORS MAKE NO
REPRESENTATIONS OR WARRANTIES WITH RESPECT TO THE ACCURACY OR COMPLETENESS OF THE
CONTENTS OF THIS WORK AND SPECIFICALLY DISCLAIM ALL WARRANTIES, INCLUDING WITHOUT
LIMITATION WARRANTIES OF FITNESS FOR A PARTICULAR PURPOSE. NO WARRANTY MAY BE CREATED OR
EXTENDED BY SALES OR PROMOTIONAL MATERIALS. THE ADVICE AND STRATEGIES CONTAINED HEREIN
MAY NOT BE SUITABLE FOR EVERY SITUATION. THE FACT THAT AN ORGANIZATION OR WEB SITE IS
REFERRED TO IN THIS BOOK AS A CITATION AND/OR A POTENTIAL SOURCE OF FURTHER INFORMATION
DOES NOT MEAN THAT THE AUTHOR OR THE PUBLISHER ENDORSES THE INFORMATION, THE
ORGANIZATION OR THE WEB SITE MAY PROVIDE OR RECOMMENDATIONS IT MAY MAKE. FURTHER,
READERS SHOULD BE AWARE THAT WEB SITES LISTED ON THIS WORK MAY HAVE CHANGED OR
DISAPPEARED BETWEEN WHEN THIS WORK WAS WRITTEN AND WHEN IT IS READ.

Note: www.state.gov is the source of much of the materials describing the Foreign Service and the Foreign Service Officer Test.

Printed in the United States of America
ISBN: 978-0-615-81137-6

Requests for permission to make copies of any part of this book should be emailed to support@FSOTreview.com.

Publisher's Note

Adar Educational Technologies is a small educational company focused on providing accurate and insightful test preparation materials for specialized exams. In 2006, Adar began offering test preparation services for the CFA Exam, a six-hour long exam given by the CFA Institute®. The CFA Exam includes several different topics, such as Economics, Finance, Statistics and Ethics. Within a short time, this review course became the best-selling CFA review course on Amazon.com.

In 2008, Adar Review recognized the need for a comprehensive preparation course for the Foreign Service Officer Test. Although there are many preparation materials in the market, none offer a comprehensive solution to prepare for the exam. Some books offer practice questions only, while others offer general test-taking recommendations but lack sufficient specific information targeted to the FSOT. The Adar Review materials were prepared by candidates who passed the CFA Exam, the FSOT and the FSOA. The principal author of the FSOT review materials recently passed both the FSOT and FSOA. This material is current as of 2013.

The purpose of this book is to provide an introduction to the FSOT, and to help you prepare for the written exam and oral assessment. Although it is not possible to provide all the information that you need to pass the exam in one volume – as a significant portion of the exam will be based on current affairs, the coverage of which is beyond the scope of this material–, we have prepared a reading list that is much shorter and more focused than the list provided by the Department of State, which we consider far too extensive to be useful in your preparation. We also provide a study guide and practice questions for the exam.

Adar Review launched its FSOT Study Guide in early 2013 and quickly became the top-selling and highest rated FSOT guide sold by Amazon. We thank our customers for making Adar Review a success. If you have any comments or suggestions on how to make this guide better, please contact us at support@FSOTreview.com.

To enhance your experience, we will be adding a blog with information about the test to our web site, a list of recommended reading materials and clickable versions of all the electronic links found in the book (so you don't need to type these long links). You can find us on the web at www.FSOTreview.com.

TABLE OF CONTENTS

Chapter I

Introduction to the
Foreign Service Officer
Selection Process

This chapter provides an introduction to the Foreign Service Officer selection process, including the Foreign Service Officer Test (FSOT), the Personal Narrative and the Foreign Service Oral Assessment (FSOA). We recommend that you read this chapter in its entirety. This chapter also provides recommendations on the Personal Narrative and other requirements of the selection process that you should review after passing the FSOT. The remaining chapters will provide recommendations on how to prepare for the FSOT and FSOA as well as provide practice questions for the FSOT.

Adar Educational Technologies congratulates you on taking the first step to become a Foreign Service Officer (FSO) and wishes you success in the Foreign Service Officer selection process. We have prepared this book to help you prepare for and succeed in this exam.

In the following pages we provide a description of the FSO career and the steps required to become an FSO. This material is current as of 2013 and the source for most of this material is from the web site of the Department of State.

Foreign Service Officer

Foreign Service Officers (FSOs) are America's advocates, promoting peace and supporting prosperity as they advance our interests and protect American citizens throughout the world. FSOs are located at over 265 embassies, consulates and other diplomatic missions in the Americas, Africa, Europe and Asia.

Please note that members of the Foreign Service <u>must be willing and able</u> to serve anywhere in the world, sometimes even in cases where family members cannot join them at their posts due to political instability or other concerns, or when family members must leave the post as conditions deteriorate. Many overseas posts are in remote countries where American-style amenities are unavailable. New FSOs are likely to be assigned to a location that is considered a hardship post. If you are unwilling or unable to live in a hardship location, you should not apply; refusal to accept a hardship position would result in dismissal from the service.

To succeed in the Foreign Service, one must be strongly motivated, enjoy challenges, and possess an ardent dedication to public service. FSOs usually share certain characteristics or traits, such as being capable, adventurous and dedicated. They also usually speak at least one foreign language and have lived or traveled extensively abroad.

In 2006, the Department of State engaged McKinsey and Company to review the strengths and weaknesses of its selections process. As a result of this work, the selection process was revised, resulting in the current examination process. As part of this process, the Department determined that it would focus its selection on candidates particularly suited to Foreign Service work. These candidates possess:
- Proven leadership skills
- Relevant overseas experience
- Solid team-building and interpersonal skills
- History of tenacity and achievement in difficult tasks

Eligibility

The Department of State requires that applicants for FSO be:

- U.S. citizens (includes naturalized citizens)
- At least 20 years old and no older than 59 years of age
- Available for worldwide assignments

Although knowledge of a foreign language is not a pre-requisite to become an FSO, proficiency in one or more foreign languages enhances your competitiveness for selection.

The Department of State hires a diverse group of candidates. For example, the orientation class of July-August 2000 included 44 new recruits, with the following characteristics:

- Age range: 22-55 (mean: 33)
- Women: 36%
- Marital status (57% single; 43% married)
- Geographic diversity: 18 different states were represented
- Education: 59% advanced degrees; 41% college degree
- Overseas experience: 61% worked overseas; 59% studied abroad
- Languages: 19 different foreign languages represented; on average each candidate spoke 1.7 foreign languages

FSO Application Process

The application process to become a Foreign Service Officer includes six steps:

(1) Career Track Selection
(2) Test Registration
(3) Written Examination
(4) Personal Narrative and Qualifications Evaluation Panel
(5) Oral Assessment
(6) Final Suitability Review & Register

The process to become an FSO is long and arduous, and it involves three major evaluations. The first one is the written examination (FSOT), the second is the Qualifications Evaluation Panel (QEP) and the last step is the Oral Assessment (FSOA). Each of these steps is very competitive and a candidate that does not pass one of these steps must take the FSOT exam again.

It is very important to prepare well for the FSOT because if you do not pass the test the first time you take it, you will have to wait 12 months before you can register to take the test again.

According to a Department of State presentation, only 8% of candidates that took the written exam in 2009 passed all three steps. This demonstrates how important it is to prepare appropriately. After passing all three steps, your name is added to the register (explained later in this chapter). Note that <u>not</u> all candidates in the register ultimately receive an offer to join the Foreign Service. In the example below, even though 778 candidates passed all three levels, the Foreign Service may only need to hire 250 new FSOs.

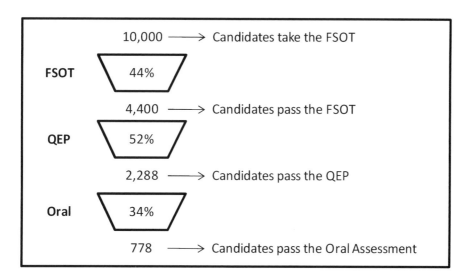

While the Department of State does not provide official figures, a 2004 article in the Washington Post stated that 19,100 people took the written exam that year (note that this was prior to the changes to the exam proposed by McKinsey). 4,400 people (23%) passed the written exam and 600-750 passed the Oral Assessment. Thus, 3%-4% of people who took the FSOT passed all three steps in 2004 and 8% passed in 2009.

<u>Important</u>: The Department of State offers information sessions and preparation sessions for the written test. These sessions are very informative and worthwhile for anyone interested in a career as an FSO. You can search for these preparation sessions at:

http://careers.state.gov/events/index.html

Choose "FSOT Information Session" from the drop down list to find the location closest to your home. Because there are so few of these sessions, you should participate in one of them even if you have not yet registered for the test.

Step 1: Career Track Selection

The first step in the process to become an FSO is to select a career track. You are urged to consider carefully which career track best fits your interests and background. This is a very important decision because <u>it cannot be changed after you start the process</u>. Also, it will affect your chances of being accepted into the Foreign Service, and will affect your career and responsibilities throughout your life at the Foreign Service.

You should be aware that, in some career tracks (political and public diplomacy) there are usually more highly qualified candidates than openings, and thus, many candidates in the register will not be hired. In other career tracks (economic, management, and consular), there may be relatively fewer candidates, thus resulting in a higher proportion of the candidates in the register being hired. While these dynamics may change over time, you should consider this information when you select a career track. If your skills and interests match multiple career tracks, you may wish to consider a career track that offers you a greater chance of getting a job offer.

Whether you want to follow a professional path that grows your management skills, impacts economic policy or helps reunite families, you'll find five different career tracks that can direct you towards realizing your goals. In order to make the most informed decision, the next section will explain the career tracks in more detail.

- <u>Management Officers</u> run the embassies and make diplomacy work.

- <u>Consular Officers</u> protect Americans abroad and strengthen U.S. border security.

- <u>Economic Officers</u> promote U.S. economic and trade interests abroad.

- <u>Political Officers</u> interpret events and situations related to U.S. interests.

- <u>Public Diplomacy Officers</u> broaden understanding of American values and policies.

We recommend that you take a 50-question evaluation at the Department of State's web site to help you determine which career track is best suited to your skills and interests. The test and additional information about the different career tracks can be found at:

http://careers.state.gov/officer/career-track.html
(click on "Which Officer Career Track is Right for You")

You should carefully read the "Guide to the Foreign Service Officer Selection Process" to learn in more detail about each of the five career tracks. This pdf file can be found at the bottom of the same web page.

http://careers.state.gov/officer/career-track.html

The Guide has a few practice questions. **<u>Do not take them at this time</u>**. Keep those questions to practice after you have studied and want to check whether you are ready for the test (approximately 2-4 weeks prior to the exam).

Management Officers
Personal characteristics: Creative, fast-thinking problem-solvers who handle diverse challenges.

Management Officers use their professional background to serve our country — meeting everyday challenges head-on while learning new skills and enjoying outstanding benefits. As action-oriented leaders, these individuals respond with efficient, on-target solutions in fast-paced and mission-critical situations.   The responsibilities of management officers include:
- Promoting leadership and professional development of staff
- Negotiating practical agreements with host countries and local businesses
- Managing multi-million-dollar real estate and other assets
- Coordinating with other U.S. agencies in embassies to work efficiently as a team
- Operating one of over 250 diplomatic posts worldwide
- Coordinating visits of senior officials

Consular Officers
Personal characteristics: Strategic thinkers and crisis managers who protect U.S. citizens and interests abroad.

Consular Officers use their problem-solving and managerial skills along with their sense of public service to address a variety of challenges facing U.S. citizens traveling, living, or conducting business abroad. As their career progresses, consular officers handle diverse challenges such as child custody disputes, arrests, travel advisories and emergencies.   The responsibilities of consular officers include:
- Working with local officials to facilitate business, educational, and tourist travel, strengthen our border security, and protect Americans
- Acquiring and applying expertise in local laws, culture, and economic and political conditions to make prompt, informed decisions affecting the lives of foreign citizens and Americans abroad

- Helping U.S. citizens with family reunification, in medical emergencies, and evacuations
- Visiting arrested Americans and ensuring access to legal counsel
- Leading a multi-cultural and highly qualified staff in developing innovative practices to protect U.S. citizens and our borders

Political Officers
Personal characteristics: Informed negotiators who interpret situations and advise on international issues.

Political Officers keep a trained eye on the political climate at their foreign posts and decipher events as they relate to U.S. interests, negotiations and policies. Political officers communicate with foreign governments to seek support for shared goals, including votes in multilateral forums. The responsibilities of political officers include:
- Developing foreign contacts in and out of politics and government to advance U.S. political interests
- Assessing the impact of political developments on the U.S. and making recommendations on action by our government
- Supporting high level visits and advising policymakers on how to communicate with foreign governments

Economic Officers
Personal characteristics: Resourceful problem solvers who build and maintain positive economic and trade relations between the U.S. and other countries.

Economic Officers work with U.S. and foreign government officials, business leaders, and opinion-makers. Economic Officers influence and implement economic and trade policy by helping unravel the complexities of a global economy. The responsibilities of economic officers include:
- Resolving market challenges, promoting fair practices, and expanding trade opportunity for the U.S.
- Working with other countries to address business, environmental and health issues
- Identifying global expansion opportunities for U.S. businesses to ensure that American entities can fairly compete for foreign investment and trade
- Researching, advising, analyzing and interpreting the economic policies and business practices of foreign countries in order to advance U.S. economic interests

Public Diplomacy Officers
Personal characteristics: Cross-cultural relationship experts who build public awareness and promote U.S. interests abroad.

Public Diplomacy Officers broaden understanding of American values and policies, and explain the breadth of American foreign policies to ensure that our positions are understood and misrepresentations are corrected. The responsibilities of public diplomacy officers include:
- Communicating with and through a variety of media to promote U.S. interests overseas
- Managing cultural and information programs
- Explaining to foreign audiences how American history, values and traditions shape our foreign policy
- Coordinating various exchange programs to strengthen relationships that improve foreign insight into American society

After selecting a career track you are ready to register for the test.

Step 2: Test Registration
To register for the test you need to go to the following web site:
http://www.act.org/fsot/

Applicants register on-line by completing an application form. This form requests factual information, such as name, address, age, education, languages spoken, work history, etc.

Registrants must submit their applications before they can reserve a test date at a test center. Test seats will be limited to 5,000 during each test window and invitations to reserve seats will be offered on a first-come, first-served basis according to when applications are received. The FSOT is offered three times per year (usually in February, June and October) during eight-day windows at numerous locations in the United States and abroad. Registrants must provide an e-mail address to receive updates about the exam. Make sure that your email spam filter accepts e-mails from www.act.org.

Applicants are informed by e-mail when they may schedule a seat for the FSOT approximately five weeks before the next test window. Because you need more than five weeks to prepare for the exam, Adar Review recommends that you start studying before you register for the test.

Important: When you receive the email from ACT asking you to schedule the exam you should immediately register for a specific date and time. If you do not schedule a time slot soon, you will not be able to make a reservation for your preferred date, time and location, and you may even lose your spot altogether. Given the frequency with which the test is given, if you miss one of the test windows you will likely need to wait four months until the next test window.

To register for the test you must first <u>create an account</u> (go to www.act.org/fsot/). You must provide the following information to create an account: Name, date of birth, social security number and contact information.

After creating an account, you will need to "launch" the registration web page and fill out a questionnaire that has several sections:

<u>Section 1</u>: Eligibility. This section requests confirmation that you meet the eligibility requirements of age, citizenship, and geographic availability.

<u>Section 2</u>: About You. This section requests biographical information including education, overseas experience and skills.

<u>Section 3</u>: Military Service. This section requests information about prior military experience.

<u>Section 4</u>: Career Track Selection. This section reminds you about the five different available tracks and asks you for your selection. As we mentioned earlier, you will not be able to change this choice. Thus, it is extremely important that you familiarize yourself with each one of these career tracks <u>before</u> you register for the test.

<u>Section 5</u>: Undergraduate School Information.

<u>Section 6</u>: Graduate School Information.

<u>Section 7</u>: Languages and Proficiency. Make sure to select all the languages you know (including those in which you have a basic level of knowledge) and properly describe your level of proficiency. Super critical needs languages (SCNL[1]) include Arabic, Chinese, Dari, Farsi, Hindi and Urdu. To qualify for SCNL, you will need to take an interview in this language. Receiving SCNL bonus points on the hiring register will require you to serve in a country where that language is spoken at least twice in your career: once during one of the first two tours, and again after reaching the mid-levels of the Foreign Service.

<u>Section 8</u>: Work Experience. Make sure to provide a good description for each job you list, including key accomplishments and specific responsibilities.

---

[1] Note that the list of critical and super critical languages changes over time. The bonus points assigned to these languages also change based on the needs of the Foreign Service.

Section 9: Other Personal Information. Includes race/ethnicity, gender and other information.

Step 3: Written Examination (FSOT)

The FSOT can be taken at ACT centers in the U.S. and select overseas locations. ACT has over 200 centers across the country that offer computer-based testing. You will likely be able to select one of several testing locations close to your home. When you receive notice from the Department of State indicating that you can register for the exam, the email will include a link to a registration page that will have a list of the testing centers located closest to your home.

You must bring the following items to the test location:

(1) Admission Letter. You must print the admission letter that you will receive by email. This letter will include your test location, date and time. You will not be allowed to take the test without it.

(2) Valid ID. You can bring a driver's license, military ID or passport. Make sure that the ID is valid (i.e., it has not expired).

(3) Bring a pen or pencil, but do not bring any paper. The test center will provide you with one sheet of paper or with a dry-erase board and marker.

(4) Forbidden Conduct. You must return all materials, including scratch paper, provided to you by the test center staff after you finish the test. You must not receive any unauthorized assistance during the test or any breaks.

(5) Dress. You should dress comfortably and be ready for an environment that may be cold (air conditioned) or warm. Thus, we recommend that you take a light sweater. Although you could theoretically dress any way you would like for the written test, we recommend that you dress in business casual attire (e.g., a sports jacket but no tie) in case the people conducting the test make notes on how you are dressed. You are applying for a job representing the United States of America; thus we recommend that you dress appropriately at the written as well as the oral assessment portions of the test. Also, ACT will take a picture of you before the test.

(6) Forbidden Items. You must not bring into the testing room any unauthorized items such as food, drinks, purses, briefcases, backpacks, calculator, cell phones, pagers, notes, books, note pads, photographic equipment, or any electronic devices. Leave these items in your car or at home.

<u>Note</u>: You are not allowed to bring a calculator and the computer you will use will have the spell check and calculator features disabled. Thus, it is extremely important that you can do simple math calculations on paper and that you minimize the number of spelling and grammatical mistakes because they will negatively affect your score.

The test should take approximately three hours and cover four separately timed sections, including three multiple choice sections and one essay section. The Foreign Service changes the length of different portions of the test and you should note that the actual test may be significantly different from the practice tests provided by the Department of State. For example, one year the Department of State web site stated that candidates would have to write one essay by selecting one topic out of two possible choices. In the actual exam, candidates were required to write two essays, one on each of the two topics.

Each of the three sections is separately timed. While taking each of the sections (e.g., Job Knowledge Test), you will be able to review and change any of the questions within that particular section as long as you do not exceed the allotted time, but you will not be able to change any of the questions in the other two sections. You will have a very limited amount of time (an average of approximately 40 seconds) to answer each question, so if you do not know the answer for one of the questions, try to quickly eliminate those choices you know are wrong and guess among the remaining choices. (You should be able to answer most questions within 30 seconds. Avoid spending more than 1 minute on any single question.) If you do not know the answer to a question, guess, write the question number on the sheet of paper (or dry erase board) and return to the question after completing all the remaining questions in the section. Since <u>you are not penalized for incorrect answers</u>, answer every single question, even if you have to guess.

Note that although you can change the multiple choice answers, you may be unable to change the written portion of the response in the biographical section. Thus, make sure that you answer accurately and completely the first time.

Although you will not be able to leave the exam room, you can select when to start each section. You should take a brief break (2-5 minutes) to relax and stretch in your chair between each of the three sections.

The multiple choice sections include the following:

Job Knowledge Test
The job knowledge test measures the candidate's depth and breadth of knowledge and understanding of a range of subjects, including:

- U.S. Government
- U.S. History
- U.S. Society and Culture
- World History and Geography
- Economics
- Mathematics and Statistics
- Management
- Communications and Computers

English Expression Usage Test
This test measures knowledge of correct grammar, spelling, punctuation and organization required for written reports and for editing the written work of others.

Biographical Information
The biographic information section assesses the candidates' prior work, education and job-relevant life experiences, highlighting attributes such as the way they resolve conflicts, interact with others, adapt to other cultures and set priorities. While this is part of the multiple choice section, some questions ask for additional written information, as explained in Chapter II.

Essay
The exam will include one or two essay statements that must be answered within 30 minutes each. The exam will make a statement and ask you whether you agree with it or not, and to support your answer. Although there is not necessarily a correct answer, you will need to analyze the problem statement and provide arguments that support your response. Important success factors include proper grammar, syntax and orthography (spelling). The software that you will use during the exam, unlike Microsoft Word, does not offer spell check and grammar check features. Thus, it is very important that you write properly.

The exam will test your ability to analyze a complex situation, but more importantly, it will evaluate your ability to quickly organize your thoughts and communicate your answer clearly and using proper English. You will also need to provide one or two facts or examples supporting your argument.

A sample topic could be about assisted suicide. The essay prompt would make a short argument for assisted suicide and a short argument against it, and then ask whether you believe that assisted suicide should be forbidden in all circumstances, in some or in none. The score on this section is more closely related to your ability to justify your answer, rather than to whether you selected the correct answer. In this example you can argue that assisted suicide is proper and should be allowed in some situations (and you will need to specify in which situations this should be allowed), or you may argue that it should never be allowed. The important factors to succeed in this section are:

(1) Take your time to think about the question and organize your thoughts.

(2) Select only one answer. If you believe that assisted suicide should be allowed in certain situations, concentrate your response on the reasons why it should be allowed – and avoid providing reasons that contradict your response.

(3) Organize your essay by first providing a short introduction and stating your thesis (i.e., your position on the question). Second, provide two or three strong arguments that support your thesis. Finally, provide a concluding paragraph that restates the thesis and elaborates on why this is the correct answer.

(4) You will need to type quickly because you will have 30 minutes to read the question, select your position, structure your essay, write it and proof read it.

(5) Avoid spelling and grammatical mistakes.

You can use the sheet of scratch paper to put your thoughts in order, but do not spend more than 5-10 minutes thinking and planning before you start typing the essay. If you wait any longer, you may run out of time before you finish the essay.

Exam Score
Within 3-5 weeks after taking the exam candidates will receive an email that directs them to a link with a letter informing them whether they passed the exam or not. This letter will only inform you of the pass/fail result, but will not provide any additional information about your results. Regardless of whether you pass or fail the test, we recommend that you request a breakdown of your scores. This breakdown will be mailed to you and it will include your score on each of the three multiple choice sections and the essay. The essay is only graded if you pass the multiple choice portion of the exam.

To receive the breakdown of your scores on the four sections of the FSOT, you must fax your request to ACT at (319) 337-1122. You must include the following information in your request: full name, address, phone number, test date, date of birth, and signature. You should receive your FSOT score breakdown in approximately 4-6 weeks by mail.

Step 4: Personal Narrative and Qualifications Evaluation Panel (QEP)

After passing the FSOT multiple choice and essay sections, you will need to submit a Personal Narrative (PN) in which you answer questions describing the knowledge, skills, and abilities you would bring to the Foreign Service. You will need to complete and submit the Personal Narrative within three weeks of receiving an email from ACT. If you pass the FSOT, you will receive an email directing you to a web site where you can complete these short essays.

This step is very important and you should not take it lightly because the QEP is one of the three steps in your candidacy and only ~50% of candidates who pass the FSOT pass the QEP. Note that the QEP reviews other information in addition to the Personal Narrative, such as scores on each of the components of the written exam, language skills and educational and work background. Thus, a high score on the FSOT (not just a passing grade) may be necessary to pass the QEP.

The Department of State describes the process as follows:
> "Although the QEP is a total file review, with no one element dominating all the factors considered, you have the most control over your responses to the PN. Your responses can be influential in determining your standing in your chosen career track. This is your chance to tell your story to the Foreign Service assessors."

While this is your chance to tell your story to the Foreign Service assessors, bear in mind that your responses are subject to verification by the Board of Examiners, and that there is a limit to how much you can write. Be concise, but try to address as many of the six "precepts" as possible. These precepts are shown on the next page.

You will have only three weeks to complete the Personal Narrative. Thus, you should think about which of your personal experiences provide the strongest example for each of the narratives you will need to write. You should do this well in advance of receiving your passing score in the FSOT so that you are not pressed for time. You do not need to finish all the Personal Narratives in one session. You can answer one PN prompt, save it in the web site and then come back another day to finish the other ones. However, you will only have three weeks to complete the PN from the time you are informed that you passed the FSOT.

The Personal Narrative will ask you to provide more details about skills you would bring to the Foreign Service, such as communications skills, ability to adapt to different cultures and leadership skills. The Department of State offers the following advice: "Focus on your own experience in answering the questions. Use these precepts as a guide to (1) give positive examples that demonstrate your abilities; (2) identify learning experiences; (3) indicate how these learning experiences will contribute to success in your chosen Foreign Service career track."

It is very important that you describe experiences that demonstrate you have the skills to be a successful Foreign Service Officer. The Personal Narrative will likely be used by the Foreign Service during the Oral Assessment, where you could be asked to provide additional details about some of your answers in the Personal Narrative. Also, note that you will need to provide references (including name and phone number) that can verify each of the questions you answer. The Department of State does not call all of these references, but they might call some of them prior to the Oral Assessment or as part of the security clearance process.

The Department of State will assess the Personal Narrative based on six precepts that are predictors of success in the Foreign Service. These precepts include:

Leadership:	Innovation, decision making, teamwork, openness to dissent, community service and institution building
Interpersonal Skills:	Professional standards, persuasion and negotiation, workplace perceptiveness, adaptability, representational skills
Communication Skills:	Written communication, oral communication, active listening, public outreach, foreign language skills
Management Skills:	Operational effectiveness, performance management and evaluation, management resources, customer service
Intellectual Skills:	Information gathering and analysis, critical thinking, active learning, leadership and management training
Substantive Knowledge:	Understanding of U.S. history/government/culture and application in dealing with other cultures. Knowledge and application of career track relevant information.

You should type all your answers in Microsoft Word first and use spell check and grammar check to make sure there are no mistakes. Once you have completed all the answers in Word, you can copy and paste the answers into the web-based questionnaire from the Department of State. Because there is a character limit (1,300 characters per question), you will need to make sure that your response in Word does not exceed that limit. You can count the characters in Word by highlighting the text and selecting Review and then Word Count. The Word Count window will tell you how many words are in your selection and will also tell you how many characters (with spaces). This number should be less than 1,300. Otherwise, your response will be truncated in the web-based questionnaire. Before you hit submit, make sure to re-read all responses to make sure that none of them were shortened by the computer due to the character limits stipulation.

Although the Personal Narrative questions may change periodically, they will likely include questions similar to many of the following:

(1) <u>Leadership Skills</u>: Leadership can be defined as motivating others, encouraging creative solutions, establishing positive team relationships, or significantly influencing the direction of the work. Describe how you have demonstrated leadership, either on one particular occasion or over time. (What was the situation? What steps did you take to show leadership? What was the result?)

(2) <u>Interpersonal Skills</u>: In the Foreign Service, you will be called upon to interact with people from different ethnic, racial, religious, geographic, economic and other backgrounds. Describe a significant experience you have had with another culture, either abroad or in the United States. (What was the experience? What did you do? What was the result?)

(3) <u>Communication Skills</u>: Communication skills are critical to successful diplomacy. Describe a situation in which you used your communication skills (either in English or another language) to further an aim or achieve a goal. (What was the situation? What steps did you take to deal with the situation? What was the result?)

(4) <u>Management Skills</u>: Foreign Service Officers are often required to manage projects, demonstrating the ability to plan and organize, set priorities, employ a systematic approach, and allocate time and resources efficiently. Describe a project you managed or helped to manage and how you sought to achieve the project's goals. (What was the project? What steps did you take to manage the project? What was the result?)

(5) <u>Intellectual Skills</u>: In the Foreign Service you may confront challenging situations that require creative use of your intellect to achieve a goal. Describe briefly how you have dealt with such a

situation in your experience using your skills of critical thinking, resourcefulness and/or judgment. (What was the situation? What steps did you take to deal with the difficulty? What was the result?)

(6) <u>Substantive Knowledge</u>: The Foreign Service seeks a diverse workforce with broad job skills and a depth of experience to represent the US overseas. Briefly describe how your education, work experience, and interests would make you a good Foreign Service Officer. In addition explain how your experiences shaped your decision to choose the career track you did.
Source: FSOA Yahoo Group

As you can see from the questions, you need to focus on actions you took and on results. It will be very difficult to answer all of these questions thoughtfully in the three-week period if you have other responsibilities (work, university, etc.). Thus, you should start working on answers to these questions as soon as you finish the FSOT written exam, and before you know whether you passed. The more time you have to answer these questions, the better your answers will be.

The Qualification Evaluation Panel (QEP) will evaluate all the information in your file, including the written FSOT examination, biographical information and the Personal Narrative to determine whether to invite you to the Oral Assessment. The QEP evaluates your file within your chosen career track, looking at how well you demonstrate the precepts outlined above. The best qualified candidates are invited to the oral assessment based on the QEP evaluation and the Department of State's anticipated hiring needs in each career track. Once the QEP review is completed, ACT will inform you of the results via email.

It is important to understand that not everyone who passes the written examination is asked to participate in the oral assessment. If you are not invited to the oral assessment you will not receive any explanation for this decision.

Step 5: Oral Assessment
After the evaluation by the Qualifications Evaluation Panel, the most successful candidates are invited to participate in the Oral Assessment, a series of exercises that constitutes the next stage of their candidacy. The Oral Assessment is conducted three times a year in the District of Columbia, San Francisco, Atlanta and Chicago. If you live in another city you will need to travel to one of these locations at your own expense. Candidates must report to their assigned Assessment Center at 7:00 a.m. on the scheduled day. The Oral Examination can take up to a full day and includes three sections: a group exercise (approximately 90 minutes), a

structured interview (approximately 60 minutes), and a case management writing exercise (approximately 90 minutes).

The Department of State offers information sessions and preparation sessions for the written test and the oral examination. You should receive an email inviting you to one of these sessions after registering for the Oral Assessment. You can also go to
http://careers.state.gov/events/index.html to search for different preparation sessions. We strongly encourage you to participate in one of the FSOA information session prior to attending the Oral Assessment.

When you are invited to the Oral Assessment you will receive an email explaining which items you need to bring on the day of the assessment. The following is a list of these items (but carefully check the email in case the list of items has changed):

- Wear a suit/business attire to the Oral Assessment, bring a nice pen or mechanical pencil and watch, take a neat block of paper and carry all the documents in a briefcase. The assessors will pay attention to your oral and written communications, but also to your overall appearance and body language. Thus, behave and dress as if you were interviewing with a top-tier law firm or investment bank.
- Valid (i.e., not expired) U.S. state or federal government-issued photo identification.
- Valid U.S. passport or original U.S. birth certificate or certificate of naturalization.
- The Social Security numbers of your dependents (i.e., those people who might be traveling abroad with you). If you don't have a passport or have an expired one, it may be a good idea to get one before the Oral Assessment.
- If you are married, engaged, married but separated, or in a romantic relationship with a cohabitant who is a U.S. citizen, a DS-7601 Spousal Release, signed by your spouse, fiancé(e), estranged spouse, or cohabitant is required. You can find a link to this form at: **http://careers.state.gov/resources/downloads**
- Prepare electronically and certify (but do not submit on line) the SF-86 Security Form. You can find a link to this form at: **http://careers.state.gov/resources/downloads**
  - o Please note that although the SF-86 asks for places you have lived and employment activity going back seven (7) years, the Department of State requires you to go back ten (10) years.
  - o Bring the printed SF-86, along with unsigned release forms generated by e-QIP, to the Oral Assessment. The e-QIP instructions can be found at:

http://careers.state.gov/resources/downloads

o <u>Statement of Interest</u>: You must bring a completed Statement of Interest (form DS-4017) to the oral assessment. You can obtain a copy of the Statement of Interest at:

http://careers.state.gov/resources/downloads

- This is your opportunity to tell the Department of State why they should hire you. Use this opportunity to tell them about your motivation to join the Foreign Service as well as what makes you a good candidate (e.g., experience working or living abroad, work or educational background, etc.) Do not worry if you repeat information provided in the Personal Narrative – this is expected.
- You can type up to 39 lines and 3,666 characters (maximum of 94 characters per line). You will want to leave a blank line between paragraphs, so you will have fewer than 39 lines of text.
- Because you are not allowed to save information on the pdf file from the Department of State web site, you need to write the Statement of Interest on a word document, where you can save it. Once you finished the document in word, you should save the pdf file from state.gov into your computer and then copy the text from your word document onto the pdf file and print it. Print several copies of the pdf file before you go to the Oral Assessment.
- Every year there are a few candidates that forget to bring a Statement of Interest or who (for a variety of reasons such as running out of printer toner) could not print it the night before and have to handwrite it at the last minute. Try to avoid procrastinating and print the statement of interest a few days before your assessment.
- The next page has a copy of the Statement of Interest (also available in our web site at www.FSOTreview.com).

• If you have a spouse, estranged spouse, co-habitant of a romantic nature, or a fiancé(e) who is <u>not</u> a U.S. citizen but who has a Social Security number, you must do the following:

o E-mail FSOAQuestions@state.gov to initiate the necessary background investigation process for this person, and complete an electronic version of the SF-85P Questionnaire for Public Trust and SF-85PS Supplemental Questionnaire for Selected Positions. Please include "Initiate Security Clearance" in the subject line of your e-mail and your partner's full name, Social Security number, and date and place (city and country) of birth in the body of the email.

- o Bring the completed SF-85P and SF-85PS, along with the associated signed release forms to the Oral Assessment. Both of these forms can be accessed via a link on:

  http://careers.state.gov/resources/downloads
- If you have a spouse, estranged spouse, co-habitant of a romantic nature, or a fiancé(e) who is <u>not</u> a U.S. citizen and who <u>does not</u> have a Social Security Number, you must do the following:
  - o You cannot use e-QIP. Print out the SF-85P and SF-85S and complete them in hard copy.
  - o Please bring the printed, signed, SF-85P and SF-85S to the oral assessment. Both of these forms can be accessed via a link on:

  http://careers.state.gov/resources/downloads

U.S. Department of State

STATEMENT OF INTEREST

FOREIGN SERVICE OFFICER

Statement of Interest

Name: _____

Please use the space below to describe why you want to become a Foreign Service officer.

Make sure that you fill out all the forms well in advance of the Oral Assessment date and that you bring them with you. Also, make sure to arrive at the assessment center no later than 6:45 AM. The Oral Assessment will start at 7:00 AM and being late makes a very poor first impression.

The Oral Assessment exercises evaluate the skills, abilities, and personal qualities deemed essential to the performance of Foreign Service Officers. The Oral Assessment measures your performance based on the following 13 criteria:

- Composure: To stay calm, poised, and effective in stressful or difficult situations; to think on one's feet, adjusting quickly to changing situations; to maintain self-control.

- Cultural Adaptability: To work and communicate effectively and harmoniously with persons of other cultures, value systems, political beliefs, and economic circumstances; to recognize and respect differences in new and different cultural environments.

- Experience and Motivation: To demonstrate knowledge, skills or other attributes gained from previous experience of relevance to the Foreign Service; to articulate appropriate motivation for joining the Foreign Service.

- Information Integration and Analysis: To absorb and retain complex information drawn from a variety of sources; to draw reasoned conclusions from analysis and synthesis of available information; to evaluate the importance, reliability, and usefulness of information; to remember details of a meeting or event without the benefit of notes.

- Initiative and Leadership: To recognize and assume responsibility for work that needs to be done; to persist in the completion of a task; to influence significantly a group's activity, direction, or opinion; to motivate others to participate in the activity one is leading.

- Judgment: To discern what is appropriate, practical, and realistic in a given situation; to weigh relative merits of competing demands.

- Objectivity and Integrity: To be fair and honest; to avoid deceit, favoritism, and discrimination; to present issues frankly and fully, without injecting subjective bias; to work without letting personal bias prejudice actions.

- Oral Communication: To speak fluently in a concise, grammatically correct, organized, precise, and persuasive manner; to convey nuances of meaning accurately; to use appropriate styles of communication to fit the audience and purpose.

- Planning and Organizing: To prioritize and order tasks effectively, to employ a systematic approach to achieving objectives, to make appropriate use of limited resources.

- Quantitative Analysis: To identify, compile, analyze, and draw correct conclusions from pertinent data; to recognize patterns or trends in numerical data; to perform simple mathematical operations.

- Resourcefulness: To formulate creative alternatives or solutions to resolve problems, to show flexibility in response to unanticipated circumstances.

- Working With Others: To interact in a constructive, cooperative, and harmonious manner; to work effectively as a team player; to establish positive relationships and gain the confidence of others; to use humor as appropriate.

- Written Communication: To write concise, well organized, grammatically correct, effective and persuasive English in a limited amount of time.

Candidates are evaluated solely against these thirteen criteria by four assessors who observe the performance of candidates in a variety of situations designed to enable the candidates to demonstrate the requisite skills. The assessors are experienced Foreign Service Officers from various career tracks. The assessors closely observe each candidate's performance, taking notes during each testing module. At the end of each exercise, assessors individually enter their scores into a computer. The average of the scores from each exercise determines a candidate's overall score. Note that each exercise and each component of each exercise are equally weighted[2]. The overall score is on a scale from 1 to 7, with 1 representing poor performance and 7 representing an outstanding performance. The passing grade is 5.25. Based on historical data, we estimate that 25%-35% of candidates pass the oral assessment.

Candidates that receive a passing score continue their candidacy. This means that the Department of State will start the background check. Although you may receive an immediate conditional offer (ICO), as the term conditional implies, this does not mean that you have an offer to join the Foreign Service. Once you receive an ICO, you will be asked to fill out forms to begin the process to obtain the medical and security clearances.

---

[2] The Group Exercise, Structured Interview, and Case Management Study each count for one-third of the total grade. Within the Structured Interview, the Experience and Motivation, Hypothetical and Past Behavior modules (see description of structured Interview below) are equally weighted.

All candidates that pass the Oral Assessment will be placed on a list of eligible hires. The list includes candidates who received a score of 5.25 and are listed in order of score (from higher to lower), using the total score including bonus points for language and veteran status.

It is very important that you obtain the highest extra points you can for language and veteran status. You can only receive one extra score for language. Thus, if you speak more than one foreign language, you should test in the one that will give you the highest extra credit. Super critical needs languages and critical needs languages provide higher bonus language points than other languages. These languages are Arabic, Chinese, Dari, Farsi, Hindi, Urdu, Korean and Pashto. (Note that the list of critical language needs, and associated bonus points, is updated regularly. Please check the web site of the Department of State for the most current list.) While the Department of State does not provide a list of extra points for each language, in previous years they gave 0.17 bonus points for passing a standard language test, 0.4 bonus points for a critical or super critical needs language (excluding Arabic) and 0.5 bonus points for Arabic. If you pass the test for French and Arabic, you would receive 0.5 bonus language points (the higher of 0.5 and 0.17), and not 0.67. The veteran's preference bonus points range between 0.17 and 0.35 and they are in addition to the language bonus points. Note that these points are bonus points. You will need to receive a 5.25 score on the Oral Assessment before you can add the bonus points. If you receive 5.20 in the Oral Assessment, you will not pass, even if you also have 0.5 bonus language points and 0.17 veteran's bonus points, for a total of 5.87 points.

The language test involves a phone call with one or two interviewers (could be on a speaker phone) in the language of your choice. They will first ask simple questions and then ask you questions involving current events. In order to pass you need to be able to discuss these topics. Note that for critical and super critical languages you do not need to have as high a level of proficiency as for standard languages. If you pass the test in one of the critical languages you will be assigned to a post in a country that speaks that language at least twice in your career.

You will receive your pass/fail score on the day of the Oral Assessment. After the assessors complete the integration of their scores, candidates are notified whether they were successful in reaching the cut-off score of 5.25. Along with their final overall score, candidates receive an indication as to whether they reached or exceeded the cut off score on any of the three major components of the exam. The passing score is based on the average score for all three sections. Thus, it is possible to fail one of the sections and still receive a passing score on the Oral Assessment.

Unsuccessful candidates are informed of their results in a private interview with two assessors. At this point, the candidate is given an opportunity to ask questions about the assessment process and future exams, but assessors are not permitted to provide specific feedback or critiques of the candidate's performance. This prevents any undue advantage to those who take the exam more than once.

Candidates who pass the Oral Assessment and receive an Immediate Conditional Offer of employment proceed to the next phase of the hiring process. At the end of the Oral Assessment, successful candidates are given a briefing on the next steps in the Foreign Service Officer Selection Process, including information on the security background investigation, language bonus point system, veteran's preference points, the medical examination, and final suitability review. Candidates are also given the opportunity to ask questions about Foreign Service life. Diplomatic Security may then initiate background interviews.

Important: You can expect to be at the Oral Assessment Center from 7:00 AM until 5:00 PM. Please plan your travel arrangements accordingly – do not get a return flight or train scheduled before 6:00 PM or 7:00 PM. (more on the schedule on Chapter III)

Anyone applying to be a Foreign Service Officer must be willing to accept the following three commitments of Foreign Service work:

o Flexibility, meaning that the candidate is willing to perform duties outside his/her functional field should the need arise.

o Public support of U.S. government policies regardless of the candidate's personal views.

o Worldwide availability. Even though the Department attempts to work with each employee's individual and family needs, each employee must be willing to serve anywhere the Department determines is necessary. This can mean in extreme climates, in isolated, potentially unhealthful and unfriendly environments, and/or where the candidate may not have training in the local language. The Department also has unaccompanied tours, where the candidate would not be able to take his/her family. These are usually one year in length, and most FSOs are likely to be assigned to at least one unaccompanied tour in their careers. There may also be tours where local conditions may force the evacuation of families back to the United States while the candidate must remain at the post.

Important: Keep these commitments in mind when writing your Statement of Interest and answering the Structured Interview questions. If your statement of interest says that you always wanted to join the foreign service to live in Europe, you are unlikely to pass the final suitability review.

Candidates who receive an Immediate Conditional Offer of employment must reaffirm orally their acceptance of these three commitments at the end of the oral assessment and in writing once a job offer has been accepted in order to continue the application process.

Step 6: Final Suitability Review & The Register

A small percentage of candidates that register for the FSOT pass the written examination, the QEP and the oral assessment (probably under 10%). If you are one of the successful candidates that receive an immediate conditional offer (ICO), you will receive information about the next steps of the registration process –obtaining medical and security clearances– before you leave the Oral Assessment Center.

Finally, after passing all these steps, you will be subject to a Final Suitability Review in which your whole file will be reviewed one more time. If you pass this review, your name will be added to the Register – this can take place up to six months after passing the FSOA depending on the complexity of the security clearance process.

The Register is a list of candidates that have passed the exam and final suitability review.   When new openings are available in the Foreign Service, candidates will be selected from the Register. The candidates on the top of the register are hired first, and many candidates that make it into the Register are never hired. After 18 months on the Register, if you were not selected, your name will be removed from the Register.

When your name is added to the Register, you will receive a letter informing you of this decision. This letter will include the name of a contact person in the Department of State; there are different contacts depending on your career track. You should contact this person by email to request an update on your position in the register and to make sure that your language points have been properly added to your exam scores.

When you are added to the Register you would receive an email with the following type of information:

"You are currently XX out of YYY candidates on the Economic register. Your ranking includes .17 language bonus points for passing the BEX Language test. Your adjusted oral assessment score is 5.67. Please note that if a candidate passes the language test, their oral assessment score is automatically adjusted by .17 language bonus points. For candidates who pass the BEX Language Test in a critical needs language, they must notify the Registrar's Office via email, that they are accepting the critical needs language bonus points and acknowledge the assignment responsibility in doing so, in order to receive the additional language bonus points."

One of the ranking criteria is your score on the Oral Assessment. Although a 5.25 is a passing score, you will likely need a higher score than that to be placed in a higher position on the register. There are three other ways to improve your score and likelihood of getting hired:

> Foreign Language: The Foreign Service assigns additional points to candidates who speak foreign languages. Speaking a common language (like Spanish or French) results in a small improvement in your position on the register. Critical languages and super critical languages (such as Arabic) will give you a more significant improvement on the register.

> Veteran or Armed Forces: The Foreign Service assigns additional points to veterans of the military.

> Career Track: Although your selection of a career track does not affect your overall score, it affects the competition that you will face, your position on the register for your chosen career track, and the likelihood that you will be hired.

Medical Clearance

The Office of Medical Services of the Department of State determines a candidate's medical fitness and ability to serve overseas. Many Foreign Service posts are located in remote areas with extremely limited medical support; therefore, each candidate must meet rigorous medical standards in order to qualify for the required worldwide medical clearance. Medical clearance determination by Medical Services is based on its thorough review of each candidate's medical history and physical examination, including an individual assessment of his/her specific medical needs and the medical capabilities of Foreign Service posts to meet those needs.

After receiving an ICO, each candidate is provided with the necessary forms to give to an examining health care practitioner. The examination will be paid by the Department of State, but if you live within fifty miles of Washington, D. C., you must have the medical examination performed at the Examination Clinic, Office of Medical Services in Washington.

Regardless of who administers the medical clearance exam, the Department's Office of Medical Services determines whether or not a candidate is medically eligible for assignment to all Department of State posts worldwide. While a candidate may effectively manage a chronic health condition or limitation within the United States or in specific areas outside of the U.S., the Office of Medical Services might well determine that this person is not eligible for a worldwide medical clearance. Such clearances may only be issued to candidates whom the Office of Medical Services deems able to serve at the most isolated and restricted overseas posts. Obtaining a worldwide medical clearance is critical to be hired by the Foreign Service.

The candidate's family (spouse and children) are also required to have a medical examination. While the candidate must be medically cleared for worldwide service, the Department of State does not consider the medical condition of eligible family members for pre-employment purposes. It does, however, require that each eligible family member have a medical clearance before they can travel overseas at U. S. Government expense when accompanying an employee on assignment.

Please note that an FSO with a family member who has been issued a limited medical clearance (not worldwide) may still be assigned to posts where that family member cannot accompany him/her. Some reasons for a limited medical clearance include chronic illnesses, pregnancy, learning disabilities or other conditions that may require treatment or facilities that may not be available at certain posts. The Department of State advises candidates to consider this situation as they pursue employment with the Department of State.

Security Clearance
Candidates who pass the Oral Assessment will have to pass a security clearance, which starts right after you pass the Oral Exam with a short explanation of the process and a finger print session prior to leaving the examination center. A comprehensive background investigation is conducted by the U.S. Department of State in cooperation with federal, state, and local agencies. This will be used to determine a candidate's suitability for appointment to the Foreign Service and to obtain the necessary Top Secret security clearance. The process considers such factors as: failure to repay a U.S. Government-guaranteed loan or meet tax obligations; failure to register for the Selective Service; past problems with

credit or bankruptcy; unsatisfactory employment records; a criminal record or other violations of the law; drug or alcohol abuse; and less than honorable discharge from the armed forces. When you are interviewed for the security clearance (and throughout the whole process) always tell the truth. It is unlikely that you will be rejected for previous drug use (unless in the past you were a heavy user, or you have used drugs recently), but you will be rejected for lying about it.

Candidates who hold dual citizenship, have had extensive travel, education, residence and/or employment overseas, or who have foreign contacts, a foreign-born spouse, immediate family members or relatives who are not citizens of the United States, should be aware that the clearance process will take longer to complete. The background investigation can include interviews with current and previous contacts, current supervisors and coworkers and your next-door neighbors. Candidates who do not receive a security clearance are ineligible for appointment. Potential candidates who have any serious issues that may prevent them from receiving a clearance should give some thought to the likelihood of their being found ineligible before starting this process.

Important: The security clearance process includes an interview with your direct manager or supervisor. Thus, your employer will learn that you are applying for a position with the Foreign Service before you are actually given an offer. That offer could take place up to 18 months after the security interview with your supervisor or may never take place – as many candidates on the register do not receive offers at all. This may be a very sensitive situation for some candidates. **Please consider this before you apply to the Foreign Service.**

If you have not received an email stating that you passed the security clearance within four months of taking the exam, send an email to securityclearance@state.gov to request an update on your security clearance. You will likely receive a response similar to this: *"You were granted Top Secret clearance on xx/xx/xxxx. Please be in touch with your HR contact for further information regarding your position."*

Final Review Panel
Upon completion of the background investigation, a Final Review Panel will examine the candidate's complete file (except medical records) to determine the candidate's suitability for employment with the Foreign Service.

The attainment of U.S. foreign policy objectives depends substantially on the confidence of the public (both American and foreign) in the individuals selected to serve in the Foreign Service. The Department of State, therefore, requires the highest standards of conduct by employees of the Foreign Service, including an especially high degree of integrity, reliability, and prudence. Given the representational nature of employment in the Service, employees must observe proper standards at all times. The purpose of the Final Review is to determine, from the candidate's total record, whether the candidate is indeed suitable to represent the United States. The Final Review Panel has the authority to terminate a candidacy.

In evaluating suitability, the Final Review Panel takes into consideration the following factors:
- Misconduct in prior employment, including marginal performance or inability to interact effectively with others
- Criminal, dishonest, or disgraceful conduct
- Misrepresentation, including deception or fraud, in the application process
- Repeated or habitual use to excess of intoxicating beverages affecting the ability to perform the duties and responsibilities of the employee's position
- Trafficking in or abuse of narcotics or controlled substances
- Reasonable doubt as to loyalty to the U.S. Government
- Conduct which clearly shows poor judgment and/or lack of discretion which may reasonably affect an individual's or the agency's ability to carry out its responsibilities or mission
- Financial irresponsibility, including a history of not meeting financial obligations or an inability to satisfy debts

The most common grounds for a finding of unsuitability are a recent history of drug or alcohol abuse and delinquency in repaying debt or other evidence of financial irresponsibility.

While the Department of State does not mention this, it is a good idea to be careful with participation in online chat rooms or social media web sites. Try to avoid inappropriate comments on sites such as Facebook or Twitter. This is good advice for any job application, and even more so for the Department of State.

The Register
After receiving medical and security clearances and passing the Final Suitability Review, your name is placed on the Register, which is a rank-ordered list of successful candidates, grouped by career track.

If you are selected for one of the Junior Officer classes, you will receive an email offering you an appointment. The email will include the following information (excerpts from an actual email):

The Registrar's Office is pleased to extend an appointment offer for the xxxx xx, 20xx - Junior Officer Class. If you are available for placement in the Junior Officer Class, please notify the Registrar's Office no later than noon, xxxx xx, 20xx. If you are available for placement in the JO Class, please provide an updated resume. Please notify the Registrar's Office of your availability for placement in the Junior Officer Class, as soon as possible.

You may receive an email like this at any time during the 6-24 months after you take the Oral Assessment. When you do, you will be given only 2-3 business days to respond. Importantly, you will need to move to Washington DC within 30-45 days after responding. Thus, you need to be prepared to accept the offer very quickly and to leave your current job with two weeks' notice. As we mentioned before, if you contact your Department of State HR representative frequently, he/she will be able to tell you your position in the register and may give you an indication of how likely it is that you will be called to serve in the Foreign Service.

If you are offered a position in a Junior Officer Class, you will not know the location of your first appointment until you complete the orientation program.

As we mentioned before, placement on the register is no guarantee of an appointment as a Foreign Service Officer because the number of appointments depends on the needs of the Foreign Service. Your name may stay in the register for a maximum of 18 months, after which it will be removed from the register. You may decline only one appointment offer before your name is removed from the register; declining a second offer will result in your removal from the register.

If your name is removed from the register, you can register to take the FSOT and begin the process again.

Assignments and Training
New FSOs begin their careers with a seven-week orientation program (A-100 course). The focus of the orientation is to introduce new employees to the structure and function of the Department of State and its role in the development and implementation of U.S. foreign policy; develop an

understanding of the terms of employment; and enhance core skills needed by all Foreign Service Officers.

The A-100 course, based at the National Foreign Affairs Training Center in Arlington, is primarily a classroom experience, but it also includes trips to Capitol Hill and to other federal agencies, as well as a three-day offsite at a nearby conference center. In addition to presentations by guest speakers and U.S. Department of State officials, A-100 also includes a series of practical exercises and case studies.

At the end of the orientation, the new Foreign Service Officers receive their first assignments, which will govern the type of specialized training that follows. That training may include public diplomacy training, consular training, political-economic tradecraft, or management training. Required language training can last for an additional six to nine months. Overall, newly hired FSOs can expect to spend from three months to one year training in Washington before their first overseas assignment.

Assignments

After orientation and training in Washington, the newly-hired Foreign Service Officer is usually assigned to an overseas post (there are a few Washington-based positions). The first two overseas assignments (usually two years each) are designed to develop the new officer's talents in different working environments and ensure that he or she has attained foreign language skills. The officer will hold a variety of positions in order to demonstrate his or her qualifications for tenure as a career Foreign Service Officer within a five-year probationary period and to see if the Foreign Service is the right fit. As part of this process, the new officer will perform two to three years on average of consular work during the probationary period, and may expect an assignment to at least one hardship post.

Hardship posts are those where living conditions are considered more difficult than in the United States. Climate, quality of local health care, crime rate, pollution levels, and availability of spouse employment opportunities are some of the factors considered in determining which locations are designated as hardship posts. Employees serving at hardship posts receive a "hardship" differential of between five and thirty-five percent of salary, depending upon the severity of the hardship. For example, in 2007, Asuncion, Paraguay received a 10% hardship differential; Bucharest, Romania 15%; and Kigali, Rwanda 25%. There is an additional incremental pay for service at a designated danger post. For example, in recent years Baghdad had a 35% danger pay as well as a 35% hardship differential.

All officers are considered worldwide available and must be prepared to go where needed.

While new officers are given the opportunity to express their preferences for postings from a list of positions available at the time of their entry into the Foreign Service, the needs of the Service remain paramount when making assignments. The Department of State takes into account personal and professional goals, training requirements, and medical and educational concerns for family members when making assignments. However, <u>some officers may not serve in positions related to their career track during the first two assignments</u>.

In particular, officers who receive bonus points for critical language skills should expect to serve in positions using their language skills in their first or second assignment. Later, as mid-career officers, they may be required to serve again in a country which uses that language skill. Even if you receive bonus points for a common language (e.g., Spanish or French) you should consider that it is likely that your first assignment would be in Spain or Latin America (Spanish), or France or Africa (French).

The need to influence the rapid pace of world change effectively requires more assignments to hardship posts where such change is occurring. Some of these positions are in danger or war zones and a good number involve sending officers without their families, who usually remain in the U.S. for the duration of the particular assignment.

As the events in Benghazi on September 11, 2012 demonstrate, the life of a FSO can be not only rewarding, but also dangerous. It requires dedication, and the flexibility to live in uncomfortable, far-away and dangerous places. This is not a career choice for most people. We commend you on your desire to join the Foreign Service and wish you success in the selection process and in your career.

Below is a list of Foreign Service locations, including embassies, consulates and diplomatic missions where you could be assigned.

<u>Africa</u>: Africa Regional Services – Paris; Angola: Luanda; Benin: Cotonou; Botswana: Gaborone; Burkina Faso: Ouagadougou; Burundi: Bujumbura; Cameroon: Yaounde; Cape Verde: Praia; Central African Republic: Bangui; Chad: N'Djamena; Democratic Republic of the Congo: Kinshasa; Republic of the Congo: Brazzaville; Côte d'Ivoire: Abidjan; Republic of Djibouti: Djibouti; Equatorial Guinea: Malabo; Eritrea: Asmara; Ethiopia: Addis Ababa; Gabon: Libreville; Ghana: Accra;

Guinea: Conakry; Kenya: Nairobi; Lesotho: Maseru; Liberia: Monrovia; Madagascar: Antananarivo; Malawi: Lilongwe; Mali: Bamako; Mauritania: Nouakchott; Mauritius: Port Louis; Mozambique: Maputo; Namibia: Windhoek; Niger: Niamey; Nigeria: Abuja; Rwanda: Kigali; Senegal: Dakar; Sierra Leone: Freetown; South Africa: Pretoria; South Sudan: Juba; Sudan: Khartoum; Swaziland: Mbabane; Tanzania: Dar es Salaam; Gambia: Banjul; Togo: Lome; Uganda: Kampala; Zambia: Lusaka; Zimbabwe: Harare; U.S. Mission to the African Union; U.S. Mission to the UN Environmental Program (UNEP)

Americas: Argentina: Buenos Aires; Bahamas: Nassau; Barbados: Bridgetown; Belize: Belmopan; Bermuda: Hamilton; Bolivia: La Paz; Brazil: Brasilia, Rio de Janeiro, Recife and São Paulo; Canada: Ottawa, Calgary, Halifax, Montreal, Quebec, Toronto, Vancouver and Winnipeg; Chile: Santiago; Colombia: Bogota; Costa Rica: San Jose; Cuba: U.S. Interests Section; Dominican Republic: Santo Domingo; Ecuador: Quito and Guayaquil; El Salvador: San Salvador; Guatemala: Guatemala City; Guyana: Georgetown; Haiti: Port-au-Prince; Honduras: Tegucigalpa; Jamaica: Kingston; Mexico: Mexico City, Ciudad Juarez, Guadalajara, Hermosillo, Matamoros, Merida, Monterrey, Nogales, Nuevo Laredo, Puerto Vallarta, and Tijuana; Netherlands Antilles: Curacao; Nicaragua: Managua, Panama: Panama City; Paraguay: Asuncion; Peru: Lima; Suriname: Paramaribo; Trinidad & Tobago: Port of Spain; Uruguay: Montevideo; Venezuela: Caracas; U.S. Mission to the ICAO; U.S. Mission to the OAS; U.S. Mission to the U.N.-New York

East Asia and Pacific: Australia: Canberra, Melbourne, Perth and Sydney; Brunei: Bandar Seri Begawan; Burma: Rangoon; Cambodia: Phnom Penh; China: Beijing, Chengdu, Guangzhou, Shanghai, Shenyang and Wuhan; Fiji: Suva; Hong Kong and Macau; Indonesia: Jakarta and Surabaya; Japan: Tokyo, Fukuoka, Nagoya, Osaka/Kobe, Sapporo and Naha/Okinawa; Korea: Seoul and Busan; Laos: Vientiane; Malaysia: Kuala Lumpur; Republic of the Marshall Islands: Majuro; Federated States of Micronesia: Kolonia; Mongolia: Ulaanbaatar; New Zealand: Wellington; Papua New Guinea: Port Moresby; Republic of Palau: Koror; Philippines: Manila; Samoa: Apia; Singapore; Thailand: Bangkok and Chiang Mai; Timor-Leste: Dili; Vietnam: Hanoi and Ho Chi Minh City; • U.S. Mission to ASEAN; Taiwan (American Institute of Taiwan)

Europe and Eurasia: Albania: Tirana; Armenia: Yerevan; Austria: Vienna; Azerbaijan: Baku; Belarus: Minsk; Belgium: Brussels; Bosnia & Herzegovina: Sarajevo; Bulgaria: Sofia; Croatia: Zagreb; Cyprus: Nicosia; Czech Republic: Prague; Denmark: Copenhagen; Estonia: Tallinn; Finland: Helsinki; France: Paris, Bordeaux, Lille, Lyon, Rennes, Toulouse,

Marseille and Strasbourg; Georgia: Tbilisi; Germany: Berlin, Düsseldorf, Frankfurt, Hamburg, Leipzig and Munich; Greece: Athens and Thessaloniki; Hungary: Budapest; Iceland: Reykjavik; Ireland: Dublin; Italy: Rome, Florence, Milan and Naples; Kosovo: Pristina; Latvia: Riga; Lithuania: Vilnius; Luxembourg; Macedonia: Skopje; Malta: Valletta; Moldova: Chisinau; Montenegro: Podgorica; The Netherlands: The Hague and Amsterdam; Norway: Oslo; Poland: Warsaw and Krakow; Portugal: Lisbon and Azores; Romania: Bucharest; Russia: Moscow, St. Petersburg, Vladivostok and Yekaterinburg; Serbia: Belgrade; Slovakia: Bratislava; Slovenia: Ljubljana; Spain: Madrid and Barcelona; Sweden: Stockholm; Switzerland: Bern; Turkey: Ankara, Adana and Istanbul; Ukraine: Kyiv; United Kingdom: London, Belfast and Edinburgh; The Vatican; U.S. Mission to International Organizations in Vienna; U.S. Mission to the EU; U.S. Mission to NATO; U.S. Mission to the OECD; U.S. Mission to the OSCE; U.S. Mission to the UN-Geneva; U.S. Mission to the UN-Rome; U.S. Mission to UNESCO

<u>Middle East and North Africa</u>: Algeria: Algiers; Bahrain: Manama; Egypt: Cairo; Iraq: Baghdad, Basrah, Erbil and Kirkuk; Israel: Tel Aviv and Jerusalem; Jordan: Amman; Kuwait: Kuwait City; Lebanon: Beirut; Libya: Tripoli; Morocco: Rabat and Casablanca; Oman: Muscat; Qatar: Doha; Saudi Arabia: Riyadh, Dhahran and Jeddah; Syria: Damascus; Tunisia: Tunis; United Arab Emirates: Abu Dhabi and Dubai; Yemen: Sana'a

<u>Central and South Asia</u>: Afghanistan: Kabul; Bangladesh: Dhaka; India: New Delhi, Chennai, Hyderabad, Kolkata and Mumbai; Kazakhstan: Astana and Almaty; Kyrgyz Republic: Bishkek; Nepal: Kathmandu; Pakistan: Islamabad, Karachi, Lahore and Peshawar; Sri Lanka: Colombo; Tajikistan: Dushanbe; Turkmenistan: Ashgabat; Uzbekistan: Tashkent

Chapter II

Foreign Service Officer Test
(FSOT)

The FSOT is composed of three multiple choice sections (Job Knowledge Test, English Expression Test and Biographical Information) and one essay section. This chapter provides recommendations on how to prepare for each of these four sections.

The FSOT is composed of four sections, three multiple choice sections which take approximately two hours, and an essay sections which takes 30 minutes. You should prepare to spend three to four hours at the test center. You can take a short break (in your seat) between each of the four sections. The test will seem to pass by much quicker than the 2.5 hours suggest.

The multiple choice sections are[3]:

- Job Knowledge Test: 60 questions in 40 minutes
- English Expression Test: 65 questions in 50 minutes
- Biographical Information: 75 questions in 40 minutes

Job Knowledge Test

The Department of State recommends that you study a number of books on history, geography, culture, grammar and other topics. The Department of State recommends that you read 10 different periodicals and 38 books.

We have prepared a shorter list of books that you must study – study, not just read – for the exam. We also have prepared a list of newspapers and magazines that you should read on a regular basis and a list of recommended books that you should read to gain additional background for the exam.

Magazines/Newspapers
You should start reading The Economist and the Wall Street Journal or New York Times on a regular basis sometime between six months and one year prior to the exam. The Economist is a must because it has articles on issues of international interest. The magazine is expensive ($160 for a year), but you can pay for your subscription using frequent flyer miles from a number of airlines or look for a recent-graduate discount (approximately $80 for a year) on the internet. In any case, this magazine is well worth the expense, and anyone interested in the Foreign Service should read it on a regular basis. You can also read articles online at www.economist.com, but we recommend that you subscribe. An interesting feature of The Economist is that it has a weekly online test on articles within the magazine. Although this is not representative of the questions you are likely to see in the exam, you should take the test every week. You can usually find this test on The Economist's main web page on Mondays or at:

http://www.economist.com/economist-quiz

---

[3] Note that the length and number of questions in each section are subject to change.

You should read all or most of the magazine every week and pay particular attention to maps. For example, the magazine published an article on the Nabucco gas pipeline in July 2009 ("He who pays for the pipelines calls the tune", July 16th 2009) that explained the proposed routes of several alternative pipelines to carry gas from Russia, the Caspian Sea and Iraq to Europe. This map is a good example of very important geographical information that you can gain from this magazine. Adar Review recommends The Economist because it has a much more global view and provides more details on foreign issues and events than Time or other American magazines.

The Department of State also recommends Foreign Affairs. Although we like the magazine and subscribe to it, we believe that its articles are too detailed compared to the questions you will find in the exam. We enjoy the magazine and recommend that you read it after passing the exam and during your career in the Foreign Service. We identified a couple of articles published in 2009 that could be useful for the exam. The July/August 2009 issue had a very interesting article about pirates, comparing those of the 16th to 19th centuries with those of current times in the Gulf of Aden. This article provided an interesting historical background (useful for the U.S. History portion of the exam) as well as information about World History and Geography. An article about the Indian Ocean in the March/April 2009 issue provided important geographical information and an interesting outlook on this most important trade route.

You should read the Wall Street Journal (www.wsj.com) or the New York Times (www.nyt.com) regularly. Although you should read all sections of the newspaper, you should focus on world news. You should also read the Sunday magazine of the New York Times.

These periodicals will provide background information about global events. You do not need to study the information from these sources, but you need to read and process the information. When you notice that one country shows up repeatedly in the news, you should study more about this country. For example, if you had taken the exam in 2010, you should have noticed that Honduras was mentioned frequently in the news in mid-2009 after its president was expelled from the country. Because this country was in the news repeatedly, you should have studied some characteristics of this country (i.e., geography and history of the country). The best sources for information are the "Country Profiles" in the Department of State's web site (and associated links such as the CIA Factbook and the Library of Congress Country Studies), and the "Country Briefs" at www.ediplomat.com. Do not use Wikipedia or other similar sources; use the sources provided in the Department of State web site or recommended in this book. You can also go to www.FSOTreview.com to see an updated list of sources with links to the relevant web sites.

In the case of Honduras, important information on which you should focus includes: original inhabitants (Mayan Indians), location in Central America, coasts (Caribbean Sea on the North and Pacific Ocean on the South), name (given by Columbus), U.S. relations (historic U.S.-owned banana plantations, one of the largest Peace Corp programs in the world). Although it would be great to learn about all the countries, you will not have time to do this. Reading the newspapers regularly will help you identify which countries to focus on.

Books
The Department of State recommends that you read 38 books to prepare for the exam. Adar Review offers a shorter list of mandatory books for the exam:
- U.S. History I (Cliffs Quick Review) by Paul Soifer and Abraham Hoffman
- U.S. History II (Cliffs Quick Review) by Paul Soifer and Abraham Hoffman
- Cliffs AP U.S. Government and Politics (Cliffs AP) by Paul Soifer
- Economics (Cliffs Quick Review) by John Duffy

You should quickly read the economics book, but you will need to study (and not simply read) the U.S. History and Government books. This is mandatory to succeed in the Job Knowledge portion of the test.

You can visit www.FSOTreview.com for a regularly updated list of recommended books and links to valuable sources of information about the Foreign Service and how to prepare for the FSOT.

These books are inexpensive and they provide the basic knowledge that you need for the exam. Highlight key terms and events and re-read them and study them during the month before the exam. Note that the Job Knowledge Test includes nine different sections:
(1) U.S. Government
(2) U.S. History
(3) U.S. Society and Culture
(4) World History and Geography
(5) Economics
(6) Mathematics and Statistics

(7) Management

(8) Communications

(9) Computers

Adar Review also recommends The Intellectual Devotional: American History by David Kidder and Noah Oppenheim. The Intellectual Devotional (under $20 at Amazon) is a valuable read prior to the exam. Unlike the two other history books, we recommend that you read (but not study) this book. This book provides a more detailed level of information than the Cliffs history books on some topics, and information on American culture, media and economics topics that may be useful in the exam.

The Dictionary of Cultural Literacy is a valuable reference, but Adar Review does not recommend it to prepare for the exam. The book has a broad scope organized in alphabetical order, which makes it very difficult to use to prepare for the exam. It also covers a wide range of information that goes beyond the materials required for the exam. The most useful sections of the book may be the business and economics section and the technology section.

The books we recommend cover information on U.S. Government, U.S. History, U.S. Society and Culture and Economics. Reading The Economist and the World sections of either the New York Times or the Wall Street Journal (in combination with the State.gov web site) should provide the necessary knowledge you require for the World History and Geography section.

It is very difficult to study for the other sections of the exam. Questions on communications and computers account for few questions in the exam, are difficult to study for and you should be able to answer many of them based on common knowledge, experience and common sense. While management may account for a larger number of questions, these questions are difficult to prepare for and you should also be able to answer based on common knowledge and experience. For further reference, we have included at the end of this chapter a short description of discrimination laws and regulations that may help you prepare for the exam.

One good source for sample questions (only 20) is the Christian Science Monitor. We found their test to be challenging.
http://www.csmonitor.com/USA/Foreign-Policy/2011/0127/Are-you-smarter-than-a-US-diplomat-Take-our-Foreign-Service-Exam/US-History

World History and Geography

Many of the questions regarding world history and geography are likely to be about countries that have recently been in the news (i.e., in the 12-18 months leading to the date of your exam). You must read about countries that are in the news to learn about their geography and history. The best place to learn about these countries is at www.State.gov. When you review this information, focus on items that are unique to the country.

Unfortunately, the Department of State has reduced the scope of its country profiles and shortened them significantly. Thus, you should supplement the information on www.state.gov with other sources, such as the CIA World Fact Book for country information (https://www.cia.gov/library/publications/the-world-factbook/index.html) and eDiplomat.com's Post Reports and Country Briefs, which include country information as well as information on local customs and the US Embassy.
(**www.ediplomat.com/np/post_reports/post_reports.htm**)

In this section, we provide some examples of countries that have been in the news over the last several years for illustrative purposes. You should focus only on countries that are in the news over the 12-18 months prior to your exam date.

Natural Disasters/Accidents
• Iceland volcano eruption (2009)
• Haiti earthquake (2010)
• Chile mine accident (2010)
• Japan Earthquake/Tsunami (2011)

Economic Problems
• Greece (2010-13)
• Ireland (2010)
• Spain (2011-13)
• Italy (2011-12)
• Portugal (2011)
• Cyprus (2013)

Political Events
• Nigeria attacks on oil supply and amnesty (2010-2011)
• Somalia pirates (2010-2012)
• North Korea leadership succession (2011)
• Iran nuclear program, Stuxnet, green revolt (2010-2013)

- Tunisia revolt and removal of president (2011)
- Egypt, Libya, Yemen and Jordan revolts (2011)
- Syria's civil war (2011-2013)
- Election of Argentinian Pope (2013)

You should prepare your own list of important countries in the news during the months preceding your exam. One good source for this is "The World This Year" section in the last annual issue of The Economist. In the 12/22/2012 issue of The Economist, the following 21 countries were listed in The World This Year:

Syria	Myanmar	Greece	Taiwan
Egypt	South Korea	Japan	Venezuela
Turkey	North Korea	France	China
Libya	Pakistan	Russia	India
Israel	Spain	Mexico	South Africa
Afghanistan			

You should consider reducing the number of countries to review to 10-15 based on the importance of the events that took place in each of them.

Below, we provide two examples: Honduras and Iceland, which were in the news in 2009 (Iceland: volcano) and 2010 (Honduras: removal of president from office). The first example includes all the information that www.state.gov provides on Honduras. We highlighted in grey the most important information – that which is unique to Honduras – as an example of how you should study about each country. The second example includes a summary of the information provided on Iceland. These are good examples of how you should prepare for the countries that you have identified as important for your exam. Also, notice when some aspects of these countries' histories intertwine with those of the U.S.

Official Name: Republic of Honduras

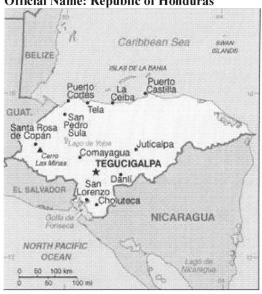

PROFILE
Geography
Area: 112,090 sq. km. (43,278 sq. mi.); slightly larger than Virginia.
Cities: *Capital*--Tegucigalpa (1,150,000); San Pedro Sula (800,000-900,000).
Terrain: Mountainous, narrow coastal plains.
Climate: Tropical to subtropical, depending on elevation.

People
Nationality: *Noun and adjective*--Honduran(s).
Population (2011 est.): 8.14 million.
Population growth rate (2011 est.): 1.88%.
Ethnic groups: 90% mestizo (mixed Amerindian and European); 7% Amerindian, 2% black, and 1% white.
Religions: 65% Roman Catholic; 35% Protestant.
Languages: Spanish (official), Amerindian dialects.
Education (2003): *Years compulsory*--9. *Primary school net attendance*--79%. *Literacy*--84%.
Health: *Infant mortality rate*--25/1,000. *Life expectancy*--72 years.
Work force (2005 est.): *Services*--39.8%; *natural resources/agriculture*--39.2%; *industry*--20.9%.

Government
Type: Democratic constitutional republic.
Independence: September 15, 1821.
Constitution: 1982; with amendments.
Branches: *Executive*--president, directly elected to 4-year term. *Legislative*--unicameral National Congress, elected for 4-year term. *Judicial*--Supreme Court of Justice (appointed for a 7-year term by Congress and confirmed by the president); several lower courts.
Political parties: National Party, Liberal Party, Innovation and Social Democratic Unity Party, Christian Democratic Party, and the Democratic Unification Party.
Suffrage: Universal and compulsory at age 18.
Administrative subdivisions: 18 departments.

Economy
GDP (2010 est., official exchange rate): $15.35 billion.
Growth rate (2010 est.): 2.8%.
Per capita GDP (2010 est., purchasing power parity): $4,200.
Natural resources: Arable land, forests, minerals, and fisheries.
Agriculture (12.4% of GDP): *Products*--coffee, bananas, shrimp, lobster, tilapia, corn, fruits, basic grains, African palm, and livestock.
Industry (26.8% of GDP): *Types*--textiles and apparel, sugar, cement, wood products, cigars, and foodstuffs.
Services: 60.8% of GDP.
Trade: *Exports* (2010 est.)--$5.879 billion: apparel, coffee, shrimp, wire harnesses, bananas, palm oil, gold, zinc/lead concentrates, soap/detergents, melons, lobster, pineapple, lumber, sugar, and tobacco/tobacco products. *Major export markets* (2009)--United States (40.9%), El Salvador (8.6%), Guatemala (7.2%), Germany (7%), Nicaragua (4.6%), Belgium (4.3%). *Imports* (2010 est.)--$8.878 billion: machinery and transport equipment, industrial raw materials, chemical products, fuels. *Major sources of imports* (2009)--U.S. (33.9%), Guatemala (10.5%), Mexico (6.8%), El Salvador (6.2%), China (4.7%), Costa Rica (4.6%).

PEOPLE
About 90% of the population is mestizo. There also are small minorities of European, African, Asian, Arab, and indigenous Indian descent. A majority of Hondurans are Roman Catholic, but Protestant churches are growing in number. While Spanish is the predominant language, some English is spoken along the northern coast and is prevalent on the Caribbean Bay Islands. Several indigenous Indian languages and Garífuna (a mixture of Afro-indigenous languages) are also spoken. The restored Mayan ruins near the Guatemalan border in Copan reflect the great Mayan culture that flourished there for hundreds of years until the early 9th century. Columbus landed at mainland Honduras (Trujillo) in 1502, and named the area "Honduras" (meaning "depths") for the deep water off the coast. Spaniard Hernan Cortes arrived in 1524.

HISTORY
Honduras was originally inhabited by indigenous tribes, the most powerful of which were the Mayans. The western-central part of Honduras was inhabited by the Lencas. These autonomous groups had their conflicts but maintained their commercial relationships with each other and with other populations as distant as Panama and Mexico.

On July 30, 1502, Christopher Columbus first saw Honduran soil and he claimed the territory in the name of his sovereigns, Ferdinand of Aragon and Isabella of Castile.

In 1523, the first expeditionary forces arrived under the command of Gil Gonzales de Avila, who hoped to rule the new territory. In 1524, Cristobal de Olid arrived with the same intent on behalf of Hernan Cortes. Olid founded the colony Triunfo de la Cruz and tried to establish an independent government. When Cortes learned of this, he decided to reestablish his own authority by sending a new expedition, headed by Francisco de las Casas. Olid, who managed to capture his rivals, was betrayed by his men and assassinated. Cortes then traveled to Honduras to firmly establish his government in the city of Trujillo before returning to Mexico in 1526. Honduras formed part of the colonial era Captaincy General of Guatemala. The cities of Comayagua and Tegucigalpa developed as early mining centers.

By October 1537, the Lenca chief, Lempira, a warrior of great renown, had managed to unify more than two hundred native tribes in order to offer an organized resistance against penetration by the Spanish conquerors. After a long battle, Governor Montejo gained the Valley of Comayagua, established Comayagua city in another location, and vanquished the indigenous peoples in Tenampua, Guaxeregui, and Ojuera.

Independence

Honduras gained independence from Spain in 1821. The country was then briefly annexed to the Mexican Empire. In 1823, Honduras joined the newly formed United Provinces of Central America federation, which collapsed in 1838. Gen. Francisco Morazan--a Honduran national hero--led unsuccessful efforts to maintain the federation. Honduras' agriculture-based economy was dominated in the 1900s by U.S. companies that established vast banana plantations along the north coast. Foreign capital, plantation life, and conservative politics held sway in Honduras from the late 19th century until the mid-20th century.

Military Rule

Authoritarian Gen. Tiburcio Carias Andino controlled Honduras during the Great Depression, until 1948. In 1955--after two authoritarian administrations and a strike by banana workers--young military reformists staged a coup that installed a provisional junta and paved the way for constituent assembly elections in 1957. This assembly appointed Ramon Villeda Morales as President and transformed itself into a national legislature with a 6-year term. In 1963, conservative military officers preempted constitutional elections and deposed Villeda in a bloody coup. The armed forces, led by Gen. Lopez Arellano, governed until 1970. Popular discontent continued to rise after a 1969 border war with El Salvador, known as "the Soccer War." A civilian President--Ramon Cruz of the National Party--took power briefly in 1970 but proved unable to manage the government. In 1972, Gen. Lopez staged another coup. Lopez adopted more progressive policies, including land reform, but his regime was brought down in the mid-1970s by corruption scandals. The regimes of Gen. Melgar Castro (1975-78) and Gen. Paz Garcia (1978-82) largely built the current physical infrastructure and telecommunications system of Honduras. The country also enjoyed its most rapid economic growth during this period, due to greater international demand for its products and the availability of foreign commercial lending.

Seven Consecutive Democratic Elections

Following the overthrow of Anastasio Somoza in Nicaragua in 1979 and general instability in El Salvador at the time, Hondurans elected a constituent assembly in 1980 and voted in general elections in 1981. A new constitution was approved in 1982, and the Liberal Party government of President Roberto Suazo Cordoba took office. Suazo relied on U.S. support during a severe economic recession, including ambitious social and economic development projects sponsored by the U.S. Agency for International Development (USAID). Honduras became host to the largest Peace Corps mission in the world, and nongovernmental and international voluntary agencies proliferated.

As the 1985 election approached, the Liberal Party interpreted election law as permitting multiple presidential candidates from one party. The Liberal Party claimed victory when its presidential candidates, who received 42% of the vote, collectively outpolled the National Party candidate, Rafael Leonardo Callejas. Jose Azcona Hoyo, the candidate receiving the most votes among the Liberals, assumed the presidency in 1986. With the endorsement of the Honduran military, the Azcona administration ushered in the first peaceful transfer of power between civilian presidents in more than 30 years.

Nationalist Rafael Callejas won the following presidential election, taking office in 1990. The nation's fiscal deficit ballooned during Callejas' last year in office. Growing public dissatisfaction with the rising cost of living and with widespread government corruption led voters in 1993 to elect Liberal Party candidate Carlos Roberto Reina with 56% of the vote. President Reina, elected on a platform calling for a "moral revolution," actively prosecuted corruption and pursued those responsible for human rights abuses in the 1980s. He created a modern attorney general's office and an investigative police force, increased civilian control over the armed forces, transferred the police from military to civilian authority, and restored national fiscal health.

Liberal Carlos Roberto Flores Facusse took office in 1998. Flores inaugurated programs of reform and modernization of the Honduran government and economy, with emphasis on helping Honduras' poorest citizens while maintaining the country's fiscal health and improving international competitiveness. In October 1998, Hurricane Mitch devastated Honduras, leaving more than 5,000 people dead and 1.5 million displaced. Damages totaled nearly $3 billion.

Ricardo Maduro Joest of the National Party won the 2001 presidential elections, and was inaugurated in 2002. Maduro's first act as President was to deploy a joint police-military force to the streets to permit wider neighborhood patrols in the ongoing fight against the country's massive crime and gang problem. Maduro was a strong supporter of U.S. counterterrorism efforts and joined the U.S.-led coalition in Iraq with an 11-month contribution of 370 troops. Under President Maduro's guidance, Honduras also negotiated and ratified the U.S.-Central America Free Trade Agreement (CAFTA), received debt relief, became the first Latin American country to sign a Millennium Challenge Account Compact with the U.S., and actively promoted greater Central American integration. While the Maduro administration implemented a number of successful economic and security policies, reliable polling data revealed widespread popular rejection of Honduran institutions, underscoring the lack of public faith in the political class, the media, and the business community.

Jose Manuel "Mel" Zelaya Rosales of the Liberal Party won the November 27, 2005, presidential elections with less than a 4% margin of victory, the smallest margin ever in Honduran electoral history. Zelaya's campaign theme was "citizen power," and he vowed to increase transparency and combat narcotrafficking, while maintaining macroeconomic stability. The Liberal Party won 62 of the 128 congressional seats, just short of an absolute majority. Zelaya's presidency was marked by a series of controversies as his policies and rhetoric moved closer in line with that of Venezuelan President Hugo Chavez. Zelaya signed on to Chavez' Bolivarian Alternative for the Americas (ALBA) in August 2008, and the treaty was ratified by the National Congress in October 2008. In the final year of Zelaya's term, he began advocating that a referendum be added to the November 2009 elections regarding reform of the constitution. Zelaya proposed that an informal poll be held on June 28 to gauge public support for his proposal. However, Honduran courts ruled that Zelaya's plans were unconstitutional and directed that government agencies desist from providing support to carry out the poll. Zelaya ignored the rulings.

Coup d'Etat

Army soldiers entered Zelaya's residence in the early hours of June 28, 2009, the day of the poll, forcibly seized Zelaya and transported him to Costa Rica. The National Congress met in an emergency session that same day, declared Zelaya was no longer president, and swore in President of Congress Roberto Micheletti as the new President of the Republic. Micheletti replaced all the cabinet members who did not accept Zelaya's ouster. As reflected in resolutions by the Organization of American States (OAS) and the United Nations General Assembly, and later in the findings of the Truth and Reconciliation

Commission, the events of June 28 constituted a coup d'etat against a democratically elected government.

Zelaya's forced removal was universally condemned by the international community, and the OAS issued an immediate and unanimous call for Zelaya's unconditional return to office. With support from the United States, the OAS designated Nobel Peace Prize laureate and then-Costa Rican President Oscar Arias as mediator to reach a peaceful, diplomatic resolution of the crisis. Through the Arias-led negotiations, the San Jose Accord, a 12-point plan for restoration of constitutional order, was drafted. The plan called for restoration of Zelaya as president, but with a consensus-based "unity government;" establishment of a truth commission and a verification commission under the auspices of the OAS; amnesty for political crimes committed by all sides related to the coup; and early elections to establish a successor as rapidly as possible. In early October 2009, negotiations were moved to Tegucigalpa and renamed the Guaymuras process. On October 30, 2009, President Zelaya and Roberto Micheletti signed the Tegucigalpa-San Jose Accord. However, President Zelaya broke off his participation in the process of implementing the Tegucigalpa-San Jose Accord after Micheletti announced on November 6, 2009, that he would form a new cabinet without Zelaya.

On November 29, 2009, Hondurans elected Porfirio "Pepe" Lobo as President in a previously scheduled free and fair election that attracted broad voter participation. Lobo received the largest number of votes for a presidential candidate in Honduran history. President Lobo was sworn in on January 27, 2010. After assuming office, Lobo formed a government of national unity and convened a truth commission, as set forth in the Tegucigalpa-San Jose Accord. Zelaya returned to Honduras on May 28, 2011, paving the way for the country's return to participation in the OAS on June 1, 2011. The Truth and Reconciliation Commission released its final report on July 7, 2011.

GOVERNMENT
The 1982 constitution provides for a strong executive, a unicameral National Congress, and a judiciary appointed by the National Congress. The president is directly elected to a 4-year term by popular vote. The Congress also serves a 4-year term; congressional seats are assigned to the parties' candidates in proportion to the number of votes each party receives in the various departments. The judiciary includes a Supreme Court of Justice (one president and 14 magistrates chosen by Congress for a 7-year term), courts of appeal, and several courts of original jurisdiction--such as labor, tax, and criminal courts. For administrative purposes, Honduras is divided into 18 departments, with 298 mayors and municipal councils selected for 4-year terms. There are no congressional or municipal term limits, but the constitution restricts the president to one term.

POLITICAL CONDITIONS
Reinforced by the media and several political watchdog organizations, concerted efforts to protect human rights and civil liberties continued up to the June 28, 2009, coup. In the immediate aftermath of Zelaya's expulsion from Honduras, the de facto Micheletti regime used troops to shut down dissenting media outlets and imposed curfews to prevent anti-coup protestors from forming large groups to voice their opposition. The de facto regime issued a decree on September 27, 2009, suspending most civil liberties and invoking a state of emergency. The de facto regime also issued an executive order giving the executive the right to close any media service it deemed a threat to national security or public order, without a court order. On October 19, 2009, the de facto regime published a decree abrogating its earlier suspension of civil liberties. The human rights situation significantly deteriorated during the de facto regime's control, with widespread reports of beatings by security forces and other abuses. In addition, the regime's movement of

security forces into the large cities, in order to maintain its rule, resulted in a significant increase in crime and drug trafficking as traditional security force activities were curtailed. Since his inauguration, President Lobo has taken important steps indicating his government's commitment to human rights, including the establishment of a Secretariat of State of Justice and Human Rights. Nevertheless, allegations of violence against and intimidation of opposition activists; journalists; and members of the lesbian, gay, bisexual, and transgender (LGBT) community continue to raise concerns regarding human rights conditions.

Organized labor is relatively strong in Honduras, representing approximately 8% of the overall work force and 13% of the apparel workforce.

Political Parties
The two major parties are the slightly left-of-center Liberal Party and the slightly-right-of-center National Party. The three much smaller registered parties--the Christian Democratic Party, the Innovation and Social Democratic Unity Party, and the Democratic Unification Party--hold a few seats each in the Congress, but have never come close to winning the presidency.

Principal Government Officials
President--Porfirio LOBO Sosa
First Presidential Designate (Vice President)--Maria Antonieta GUILLEN de BOGRAN
Secretary of State of Foreign Relations--Alden RIVERA (Interim)
President of Congress--Juan Orlando HERNANDEZ
Ambassador to the United States--Jorge Ramon Hernandez-Alcerro
Ambassador to the United Nations--Mary Elizabeth FLORES Flake
Ambassador to the OAS--Jorge Ramon Hernandez-Alcerro

Honduras maintains an embassy in the United States at 3007 Tilden Street NW, Washington, DC 20008 (tel. 202-966-7702). For more information concerning entry and exit requirements, travelers may contact the Consular office at 1014 M Street NW, Washington, DC 20001; telephone (202) 682-5948; e-mail: **consulado.washington@hondurasemb.org**. Honduras also has consulates in Atlanta, Chicago, Houston, Miami, Los Angeles, New Orleans, New York, Phoenix, and San Francisco and an Honorary Consul in San Juan, Puerto Rico. For tourist information or suggestions, please contact the Honduras Institute of Tourism at 1-800-410-9608 (in the United States) or at 1-800-222-TOUR (8687) (within Honduras only) or visit the web site at **http://www.iht.hn/?q=contactos**.

ECONOMY
Honduras, with an estimated per capita gross domestic product (GDP) of $4,200 in 2010 (PPP), is one of the poorest countries in the western hemisphere, with about 65% of the population living in poverty. While 2010 estimates project GDP to have grown by 2.8%, Honduras' GDP fell by 2.1% in 2009. Reasons for this contraction included the worldwide economic downturn and the political crisis surrounding the forced removal of President Zelaya from power. Previously, the economy grew by more than 6% per year from 2004 to 2007, and by 4% in 2008.

Historically dependent on exports of agricultural goods, the Honduran economy has diversified in recent decades and now has a strong export-processing (maquila) industry, primarily focused on assembling textile and apparel goods for re-export to the United States, as well as automobile wiring harnesses and similar products. Despite the recent economic diversification, there continues to be a large subsistence farming population with few economic opportunities. Honduras also has extensive forest, marine, and mineral resources, although widespread slash-and-burn agricultural methods and illegal logging continue to destroy Honduran forests.

Because of a strong commercial relationship with the United States, Honduras was hit hard by the international economic downturn, especially in the maquila industry, where orders were estimated to have declined about 40%, and where about 30,000 workers lost their jobs in 2008 and 2009 out of a pre-crisis workforce of 145,000. The maquila sector began to see an upswing toward the end of 2009 as the U.S. economy stabilized, and it has begun re-expanding its employment base. Over one-third of the Honduran workforce was considered either unemployed or underemployed in 2010.

Roughly 1 million Hondurans have migrated to the United States. Remittance inflows from Hondurans living abroad, mostly in the United States, are the largest source of foreign income and a major contributor to domestic demand. Remittances totaled $2.8 billion in 2009, down 11.8% from 2008 levels; that is equivalent to about one-fifth of Honduras' GDP.

NATIONAL SECURITY
With the cessation of the 1980s civil wars in El Salvador and Nicaragua, the Honduran armed forces refocused their orientation toward combating transnational threats such as narcoterrorism and organized crime. Honduras supports efforts at regional integration and deployed troops to Iraq in support of Operation Iraqi Freedom. In 1999, the constitution was amended to abolish the position of military commander in chief of the armed forces, thus codifying civilian authority over the military.

FOREIGN RELATIONS
Honduras is a member of the United Nations, the World Trade Organization (WTO), the Organization of American States (OAS), the Central American Parliament (PARLACEN), the Central American Integration System (SICA), the Conference of Central American Armed Forces (CFAC), and the Central American Security Commission (CASC). Honduras is also a signatory to the Rio Pact, and a member of the Central American Defense Council (CONDECA). During 1995-96, Honduras--a founding member of the United Nations--served as a nonpermanent member of the UN Security Council for the first time. Honduras is a party to all UN and OAS counterterrorism conventions and protocols.

Honduras is a strong proponent of Central American cooperation and integration, and before the June 2009 coup was working toward the implementation of a regional customs union and Central American passport, which would ease border controls and tariffs among Honduras, Guatemala, Nicaragua, and El Salvador.

In 1969, El Salvador and Honduras fought the brief "Soccer War" over disputed border areas. The two countries formally signed a peace treaty in 1980, which put the border dispute before the International Court of Justice (ICJ). In 1992, the IJC awarded most of the disputed territory to Honduras, and in January 1998, Honduras and El Salvador signed a border demarcation treaty to implement the terms of the ICJ decree, although delays continue due to technical difficulties. However, Honduras and El Salvador maintain normal diplomatic and trade relations. Honduras also has unresolved maritime border disputes with El Salvador, Jamaica, and Cuba.

U.S.-HONDURAN RELATIONS
Overview
Honduras has traditionally been an ally of the United States and generally supports U.S. initiatives in international fora. There was close cooperation with Honduras in the areas of counternarcotics and counterterrorism before June 2009, but because the de facto regime was not recognized as the legitimate government, these activities were suspended. The U.S. recognized the November 2009 presidential election and is cooperating with the Lobo administration to combat poverty, to improve education and health standards for all Hondurans, to strengthen the rule of law and respect for human rights, and to increase Honduras' ability to fight transnational crime and provide a safe environment for all of its citizens. Honduras was among the first countries to sign an International Criminal Court (ICC) Article 98 Agreement with the U.S., and the Honduran port of Puerto Cortes is part of the U.S. Container Security Initiative (CSI). Honduras was also the first Central American country to sign a letter of agreement (LOA) to implement the Merida Initiative, now known as the Central American Regional Security Initiative (CARSI).

During the 1980s, Honduras supported U.S. policy opposing a revolutionary Marxist government in Nicaragua and an active leftist insurgency in El Salvador. The Honduran Government also played a key role in negotiations that culminated in the 1990 Nicaraguan elections. Honduras continues to participate in the UN observer mission in the Western Sahara, contributed 370 troops for stabilization in Iraq, and remains interested in participating in other UN peacekeeping missions.

In 2004, the United States signed the U.S.-Central America Free Trade Agreement (CAFTA) with Honduras, El Salvador, Nicaragua, Guatemala, Costa Rica, and the Dominican Republic. The legislatures of all signatories except Costa Rica ratified CAFTA in 2005, and the agreement entered into force in the first half of 2006. CAFTA eliminates tariffs and other barriers to trade in goods, services, agricultural products, and investments. Additionally, CAFTA is expected to solidify democracy, encourage greater regional integration, and provide safeguards for environmental protection and labor rights. The United States is Honduras' chief trading partner and the largest investor in Honduras.

The United States maintains a small presence at a Honduran military base; until suspension as a result of the June 2009 coup, the two countries conducted joint peacekeeping, counternarcotics, humanitarian, disaster relief, and civic action exercises. U.S. troops conduct and provide logistics support for a variety of bilateral and multilateral exercises--medical, engineering, peacekeeping, counternarcotics, and disaster relief--for the benefit of the Honduran people and their Central American neighbors. U.S. forces--regular, reserve, and National Guard--benefit greatly from these exercises. These activities resumed once constitutional government was restored.

U.S. Policy Toward Honduras
U.S. policy toward Honduras is aimed at consolidating democracy, protecting human rights, and promoting the rule of law, and U.S. policy regarding the June 2009 coup pursued those aims. U.S. Government programs are aimed at promoting a healthy and more open economy capable of sustainable growth, improving the climate for business and investment while protecting U.S. citizen and corporate rights, and promoting the well-being of the Honduran people. The United States also works with Honduras to meet transnational challenges--including the fight against terrorism, narcotics trafficking, money laundering, illegal migration, and trafficking in persons--and encourages and supports Honduran efforts to protect the environment. The goals of strengthening democracy and promoting viable economic growth are especially important given the geographical proximity of Honduras to the United States. An estimated 1 million

Hondurans reside in the United States, 600,000 of whom are believed to be undocumented; consequently, immigration issues are an important item on the bilateral agenda.

U.S.-Honduras ties are further strengthened by numerous private sector contacts, with an average of between 80,000 and 110,000 U.S. citizens visiting Honduras annually and about 15,000 Americans residing there. More than 200 American companies operate in Honduras.

Economic and Development Assistance
In order to help strengthen Honduras' democratic institutions and improve living conditions, the United States has provided substantial economic assistance. The United States has historically been the largest bilateral donor to Honduras. The planned USAID budget for Honduras is $53.2 million for fiscal year 2011. Over the years, U.S. foreign assistance has helped advance such objectives as fostering democratic institutions, improving education and the health status of the population, increasing private sector employment and income, helping Honduras manage its arrears with international financial institutions, providing humanitarian aid, increasing agricultural production, and providing loans to microbusinesses.

1998's Hurricane Mitch left hundreds of thousands homeless, devastated the road network and other public infrastructure, and crippled key sectors of the economy. Estimates show that Hurricane Mitch caused $8.5 billion in damages to homes, hospitals, schools, roads, farms, and businesses throughout Central America, including more than $3 billion in Honduras alone. In response, the United States provided more than $461 million in immediate disaster relief and humanitarian aid over the years 1998-2001. This supplemental assistance was designed to help repair water and sanitation systems; replace housing, schools, and roads; provide agricultural inputs; provide local government crisis management training; grant debt relief; and encourage environmental management expertise. Additional resources were utilized to maintain anti-crime and drug assistance programs.

In June 2005, Honduras became the first country in the hemisphere to sign a Millennium Challenge Account (MCA) Compact with the U.S. Government. Under the Compact, the U.S. Millennium Challenge Corporation invested $205 million over 5 years to help Honduras improve its road infrastructure, diversify its agriculture, and transport its products to market.

The Peace Corps has been active in Honduras since 1962, and currently the program is one of the largest in the world. In 2009, there were approximately 180 Peace Corps Volunteers working in the poorest parts of Honduras. Volunteers work in six project areas including: HIV/AIDS Prevention and Child Survival, Youth Development, Protected Areas Management, Business, Water and Sanitation, and Municipal Development.

The U.S. Government strongly supports the professionalization of the civilian police force as an important element in strengthening the rule of law in Honduras. The American Embassy in Tegucigalpa provides specialized training to police officers.

Security Assistance
The role of the Honduran armed forces has changed significantly in recent years as many institutions formerly controlled by the military are now under civilian authority. The annual defense and police budgets are approximately $75 million with very modest increases in the past few years. Prior to the June 28, 2009, political crisis, Honduras

received modest U.S. security assistance funds and training. During the coup regime, there was no official U.S.-Honduran military interaction.

Historically, in the absence of a large security assistance program, defense cooperation has taken the form of increased participation by the Honduran armed forces in military-to-military contact programs and bilateral and multilateral combined exercises oriented toward peacekeeping, disaster relief, humanitarian/civic assistance, and counternarcotics. The U.S. Joint Task Force Bravo (JTF-Bravo), stationed at the Honduran Soto Cano Air Base, plays a vital role in supporting combined exercises in Honduras and in neighboring Central American countries. JTF-Bravo plays a critical role in helping the United States respond to natural disasters in Central America by serving as a platform for rescue missions, repairing critical infrastructure, and in meeting high priority health and sanitation needs. JTF-Bravo forces have helped deliver millions of dollars worth of privately donated goods to those in need. JTF-Bravo also provides logistical support to interagency partners in the region that combat illegal trafficking activities.

U.S. Business Opportunities

The U.S. is the chief trading partner for Honduras, supplying 34% of Honduran imports and purchasing 41% of Honduran exports in 2010. Bilateral trade between the two nations totaled $8.3 billion in 2010. U.S. exports to Honduras in 2010 totaled $4.6 billion, a 36.8% increase from 2009. U.S. imports from Honduras rose 18.4% from the implementation of CAFTA until 2009, while U.S. exports to Honduras grew by 48.9% in that period.

CAFTA eliminates most tariffs and other barriers for U.S. goods destined for the Central American market, provides protection for U.S. investments and intellectual property, and creates more transparent rules and procedures for conducting business. CAFTA also aims to eliminate intra-Central American tariffs and facilitate increased regional trade, benefiting U.S. companies manufacturing in Honduras. With CAFTA implemented, about 80% of U.S. goods now enter the region duty-free, with tariffs on the remaining 20% to be phased out by 2016.

Leading U.S. exports in 2009 included: textile yarn and fabric, petroleum and petroleum products, cereals and cereal preparations, low-value shipments, and apparel. Nearly all textile and apparel goods that meet CAFTA's rules of origin became duty-free and quota-free immediately, thus promoting new opportunities for U.S. fiber, yarn, fabric, and apparel manufacturers. Honduras is the seventh-largest exporter of apparel and textile products by volume to the U.S. market behind countries such as Mexico and China; Honduras is first among Central American and Caribbean countries.

The stock of U.S. foreign direct investment in Honduras rose 7.2% between 2008 and 2009, from $787 million to $844 million. This was concentrated largely in the manufacturing, finance, insurance, and banking sectors of the country.

For further information on investing in Honduras, please review the State Department's Investment Climate Statement.

Principal U.S. Embassy Officials
Ambassador--Lisa Kubiske
Deputy Chief of Mission--Matthias Mitman
Political Counselor--Silvia Eiriz
Economic Counselor--Mary Grace McGeehan
USAID Director--William Brands

Public Diplomacy Counselor--Stephen J. Posivak
Consul General--William D. Douglass
Defense Attache--Col. Robert W. Swisher
Military Group Commander--Col. Jeffrey E. Blalock
Peace Corps Country Director--Emily Untermeyer

The U.S. Embassy in Honduras is located on Avenida La Paz, Tegucigalpa (tel.: 011-504-2236-9320; faxes: general--011-504-2236-9037, USAID--011-504-2236-7776, Consulate--011-504-2238-4357). Internet: http://honduras.usembassy.gov/.

Contact Information
American Chamber of Commerce (AMCHAM)
Hotel Honduras Maya
Apartado Postal 1838
Tegucigalpa, Honduras
Tel: +504 2231-1379/2232-6035
Fax: +504 232-2031
Branch office in San Pedro Sula
Tel: +504 2557-6412/2557-7634
Fax: +504 2557-6402

U.S. Department of Commerce
International Trade Administration
Office of Latin America and the Caribbean
14th and Constitution Avenue, NW
Washington, DC 20230
Tel: 202-482-0057
800-USA-TRADE
Fax: 202-482-0464
Internet: http://www.export.gov

U.S. Agency for International Development
1300 Pennsylvania Avenue, NW
Washington, DC 20523-0001
Tel: 202-712-4810
Fax: 202-216-3524
Internet: http://www.
usaid.gov

TRAVEL AND BUSINESS INFORMATION
Travel Alerts, Travel Warnings, Trip Registration
The U.S. Department of State's Consular Information Program advises Americans traveling and residing abroad through Country Specific Information, Travel Alerts, and Travel Warnings. Country Specific Information exists for all countries and includes information on entry and exit requirements, currency regulations, health conditions, safety and security, crime, political disturbances, and the addresses of the U.S. embassies and consulates abroad. Travel Alerts are issued to disseminate information quickly about terrorist threats and other relatively short-term conditions overseas that pose significant risks to the security of American travelers. Travel Warnings are issued when the State

Department recommends that Americans avoid travel to a certain country because the situation is dangerous or unstable.

For the latest security information, Americans living and traveling abroad should regularly monitor the Department's Bureau of Consular Affairs Internet web site at http://travel.state.gov, where current Worldwide Caution, Travel Alerts, and Travel Warnings can be found. The travel.state.gov website also includes information about passports, tips for planning a safe trip abroad and more. More travel-related information also is available at http://www.usa.gov/Citizen/Topics/Travel/International.shtml.

The Department's Smart Traveler app for U.S. travelers going abroad provides easy access to the frequently updated official country information, travel alerts, travel warnings, maps, U.S. embassy locations, and more that appear on the travel.state.gov site. Travelers can also set up e-tineraries to keep track of arrival and departure dates and make notes about upcoming trips. The app is compatible with iPhone, iPod touch, and iPad (requires iOS 4.0 or later).

The Department of State encourages all U.S. citizens traveling or residing abroad to register via the State Department's travel registration website or at the nearest U.S. embassy or consulate abroad (a link to the registration page is also available through the Smart Traveler app). Registration will make your presence and whereabouts known in case it is necessary to contact you in an emergency and will enable you to receive up-to-date information on security conditions.

Emergency information concerning Americans traveling abroad may be obtained by calling 1-888-407-4747 toll free in the U.S. and Canada or the regular toll line 1-202-501-4444 for callers outside the U.S. and Canada.

Passports

The National Passport Information Center (NPIC) is the U.S. Department of State's single, centralized public contact center for U.S. passport information. Telephone: 1-877-4-USA-PPT (1-877-487-2778); TDD/TTY: 1-888-874-7793. Passport information is available 24 hours, 7 days a week. You may speak with a representative Monday-Friday, 8 a.m. to 10 p.m., Eastern Time, excluding federal holidays.

Health Information

Travelers can check the latest health information with the U.S. Centers for Disease Control and Prevention in Atlanta, Georgia. A hotline at 800-CDC-INFO (800-232-4636) and a web site at http://wwwn.cdc.gov/travel/default.aspx give the most recent health advisories, immunization recommendations or requirements, and advice on food and drinking water safety for regions and countries. The CDC publication "Health Information

for International Travel" can be found at
http://wwwn.cdc.gov/travel/contentYellowBook.aspx.

More Electronic Information
Department of State Web Site. Available on the Internet at http://www.state.gov, the
Department of State web site provides timely, global access to official U.S. foreign policy
information, including more Background Notes, the Department's daily press briefings
along with the directory of key officers of Foreign Service posts and more. The Overseas
Security Advisory Council (OSAC) provides security information and regional news that
impact U.S. companies working abroad through its website http://www.osac.gov

---

As you can see, the Department of State offers almost 14 pages of information on
Honduras, far too extensive to be useful for the exam. However, after a quick read, you
can summarize certain facts about the country. Make sure that you examine the map to
gain any important information about the country. Also, look at the country's location in
a larger regional or world map.

Map Facts:
- Honduras has access to the Caribbean Sea (and Atlantic Ocean) and to the Pacific
  Ocean.
- The Caribbean is on the North of the country and the Pacific is on the South.
- From World Map: Honduras is in the Northern Hemisphere, approximately $13°$- $16°$
  North of the Equator (South of the Tropic of Cancer).

Some highlighted facts:
- Honduras was originally inhabited by indigenous tribes, the most powerful of which
  were the Mayans.
- The restored Mayan ruins near the Guatemalan border in Copan reflect the great
  Mayan culture that flourished there for hundreds of years until the early 9th century.
- Columbus landed at mainland Honduras (Trujillo) in 1502, and named the area
  "Honduras" (meaning "depths") for the deep water off the coast.
- Honduras gained independence from Spain in 1821. The country was then briefly
  annexed to the Mexican Empire.
- Honduras' agriculture-based economy was dominated in the 1900s by U.S. companies
  that established vast banana plantations along the north coast.
- Roughly 1 million Hondurans have migrated to the United States.
- Remittance inflows from Hondurans living abroad are the largest source of foreign
  income. Remittances totaled $2.8 billion in 2009, equivalent to about one-fifth of
  Honduras' GDP.
- In 1969, El Salvador and Honduras fought the brief "Soccer War" over disputed
  border areas.

- In 2004, the United States signed the U.S.-Central America Free Trade Agreement (CAFTA) with Honduras, El Salvador, Nicaragua, Guatemala, Costa Rica, and the Dominican Republic.
- The United States is Honduras' chief trading partner and the largest investor in Honduras.
- The United States maintains a small presence at a Honduran military base.
- The Peace Corps has been active in Honduras since 1962, and currently the program is one of the largest in the world. In 2009, there were approximately 180 Peace Corps Volunteers working in the poorest parts of Honduras. Volunteers work in six project areas including: HIV/AIDS Prevention and Child Survival, Youth Development, Protected Areas Management, Business, Water and Sanitation, and Municipal Development.

Based on this information, if Honduras was in the news again, you may see a question similar to this:

Question: The following Central American country has ports on the Caribbean and Pacific coasts. The country was inhabited by Mayan Indians and was discovered and named by Columbus in 1502. After gaining its independence from Spain, this country was briefly part of the Mexican Empire. The Peace Corps has been active in this country since 1962 and currently the program is one of the largest in the world. Which of the following countries meets this description?

(1) El Salvador
(2) Cuba
(3) Honduras
(4) Panama

Answer: Even if you do not know much about this country, you can easily remove Cuba because it is a Caribbean island without a port on the Pacific coast. You may also be able to remove El Salvador because it does not have a Caribbean Coast. Also, El Salvador was inhabited by Aztec rather than Mayan Indians. El Salvador was discovered by Spain in 1522. If you had read the country profile for Honduras, you would very quickly realize that this is the correct answer.

(We shortened the description of Iceland to show you the parts that you should read)

OFFICIAL NAME: Republic of Iceland

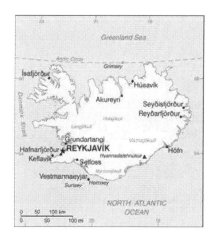

Geography

Area: About the size of Virginia or slightly larger than Ireland.
Cities: *Capital*--Reykjavík (pop. 117,898).
Climate: Maritime temperate.

People

Population (January 1, 2009): 319,368.
Ethnic group: Relatively homogenous mixture of descendants of Norwegians and Celts.
Religion: Evangelical Lutheran, 86%. Language: Icelandic.

Government

Type: Semi-presidential, parliamentary.
Independence: 1918 (became "sovereign state" under Danish Crown); 1944 Full
independence (establishment of republic).

Economy

GDP (2008): $12.1 billion. GDP growth rate: (2006) 4.2%; (2007) 3.8%; (2008) 0.3%.
Per capita GDP (2008): $52,088.
Inflation rate: (2007) 5.1%; (January 2009) 18.6%; (March 2009) 15.9%.
Net central government debt: (2007) 4.4% of GDP; (2008) 27.8% of GDP; (2009 -
predicted) 57.8% of GDP.
Natural resources: Marine products, hydroelectric and geothermal power.

Trade

Exports (2007)--$4.8 billion: marine products 41.8%; industrial products 38.9%
Partners (2008)--EEA 80.6% (Netherlands 34.3%, Germany 11.4%, U.K. 11.6%, Ireland
0.3%, Spain 3.8%, Norway 4.4%, Denmark 3.1%); U.S. 5.5% ($250 million); Japan
4.4%.

Imports (2007)--$6.7 billion: industrial supplies 26.7%; capital goods, parts, accessories 21.5%; consumer goods 15.7%; transport equipment 20.5%
Partners (2008)--EEA 64.8% (Germany 10.3%, Sweden 9%, Denmark 7.3%, Netherlands 6.1%, U.K. 4.4%, Norway 11.2%, Switzerland 3.2%, Italy 2.8%); U.S. 8.0% ($341 million); Japan 3.7%.

GEOGRAPHY
Iceland is a volcanic island in the North Atlantic Ocean east of Greenland and immediately south of the Arctic Circle. About 79% of Iceland's land area, which is of recent volcanic origin, consists of glaciers, lakes, a mountainous lava desert (highest elevation 2,000 meters--6,590 ft.--above sea level), and other wasteland. The inhabited areas are on the coast, particularly in the southwest where about 60% of the population lives. Because of the Gulf Stream's moderating influence, the climate is characterized by damp, cool summers and relatively mild but windy winters. In Reykjavík, the average temperature is 11°C (52°F) in July and -1°C (30°F) in January.

PEOPLE
According to Icelandic Government statistics, 93% of the nation's inhabitants live in urban areas and about 60% live in the Reykjavík metropolitan area.

HISTORY
Iceland was settled in the late 9th and early 10th centuries, principally by people of Norse origin. In 930 A.D., the ruling chiefs established a republican constitution and an assembly called the Althingi (Alþingi) the oldest parliament in the world. Iceland remained independent until 1262, when it entered into a treaty establishing a union with the Norwegian monarchy. Iceland passed to Denmark in the late 14th century when Norway and Denmark were united under the Danish crown.

Iceland became a charter member of the North Atlantic Treaty Organization (NATO) in 1949. Iceland is the only NATO country with no standing military of its own.

POLITICAL CONDITIONS
When the Icelandic banking sector collapsed in fall 2008, taking the nation's economy with it, opinion polls showed less than 50% of the public had confidence in the government's crisis management. The resulting protests were Iceland's most serious since the riots over NATO membership in 1949. Iceland's current political uncertainty follows nearly two decades of relative stability. Longtime IP leader Davíð Oddsson was Prime Minister 1991-2004, making him the longest-serving prime minister in Europe.

Following the economic collapse of 2008, the government undertook a thorough review of its policy on joining the EU, concluding that the question should be decided by national referendums before and at the conclusion of membership talks with Brussels.

ECONOMY

Iceland, a stable democracy with a dynamic consumer economy, suffered an economic meltdown in October 2008. The banking sector collapsed and the Icelandic Government turned to the International Monetary Fund (IMF) for assistance. This was a marked change from the economic boom Iceland had experienced from several years of strong economic growth spurred by economic reforms, deregulation, and low inflation, averaging around 4%. The economy suffered an initial setback in spring 2006 when credit rating agencies and other international financial firms released a number of reports raising questions about the activities and stability of Iceland's major banks and the state of the Icelandic economy. These reports were widely covered in the international financial press, causing a marked drop in the value of shares listed on the Icelandic stock exchange and of the Icelandic krona, but the market recovered as reforms were made in the banking sector. Then the financial sector was hit hard by the global credit crisis beginning in 2007. Although Icelandic banks had limited sub-prime mortgage market exposure, they were affected by the general lack of available capital. In the first six months of 2008, the Icelandic krona began devaluing and inflation rose to nearly 12%. Difficulties increased as Icelandic banks were not able to get financing on the global market and they were forced to turn to their lender of last resort, the Central Bank of Iceland. In October 2008, the Central Bank bailed out one major bank, but then a week later took possession of the three largest banks. This set off the financial crisis as the size of the banks' liabilities were estimated to be multiple times GDP. Iceland turned to the IMF for a $5.1 billion loan package that included bilateral loans from the Nordics and other countries. The long-term ramifications of the financial crisis are still developing, but so far have resulted in a dramatic rise in unemployment from less than 2% to 10.5% and widespread business closures and bankruptcies. Political turmoil resulted in the resignation of the cabinet and installation of an interim government as well as the replacement of the Central Bank and Financial Supervisory Authority leadership. At the end of 2008, inflation was at a rate of 18.6% and the currency had depreciated by roughly 90%.

Traditionally marine products have accounted for the majority of Iceland's exports of goods, but for the first time ever, in 2008 aluminum exports exceeded marine product exports. The vast majority of Iceland's exports go to the European Union (EU) and the European Free Trade Association (EFTA) countries, followed by the United States and Japan. The U.S. is by far the largest foreign investor in Iceland. A Trade and Investment Framework Agreement (TIFA) with the United States was signed in January 2009.

Iceland has no railroads. Organized road building began about 1900 and has greatly expanded in the past decade. The current national road system connects most of the population centers along the coastal areas and consists of about 13,000 kilometers (8,125 mi.) of roads, of which about 4,800 kilometers (2,982 mi.) are paved. Regular air and sea service connects Reykjavík with the other main population centers.

DEFENSE

The U.S. and Iceland signed a bilateral agreement in 1951 stipulating that the U.S. would make arrangements for Iceland's defense on behalf of NATO and providing for basing rights for U.S. forces in Iceland. In March 2006 the U.S. announced it would continue to provide for Iceland's defense but without permanently basing forces in the country; Naval Air Station Keflavík closed in September 2006 after 55 years.

FOREIGN RELATIONS

Iceland maintains diplomatic and commercial relations with practically all nations, but its ties with other Nordic states, with the United States, and with the other NATO member states are particularly close. Icelanders remain especially proud of the role Iceland played in hosting the historic 1986 summit in Reykjavík between President Reagan and Soviet leader Gorbachev, which set the stage for the end of the Cold War.

Icelanders have a strong emotional bond with the Baltic states, and Iceland prides itself on being the first country to have recognized these countries' claim for independence in 1991.

Membership in International Organizations

Iceland is a member of the following organizations: European Economic Area; European Free Trade Organization; North Atlantic Treaty Organization; Organization for Security and Cooperation in Europe; Organization for Economic Cooperation and Development; It also is a member of the United Nations and most of its related organizations, specialized agencies, and commissions, including the International Monetary Fund and World Trade Organization

U.S.-ICELANDIC RELATIONS

U.S. policy aims to maintain close, cooperative relations with Iceland, both as a NATO ally and as a friend interested in the shared objectives of enhancing world peace; respect for human rights; economic development; arms control; and law enforcement cooperation, including the fight against terrorism, narcotics, and human trafficking. Moreover, the United States endeavors to strengthen bilateral economic and trade relations.

Below is a summary of important facts about the country.

Map Facts:
- Island nation located in the North Atlantic Ocean.
- Located just south of the Arctic Circle.

Some highlighted facts:
- Population about 300,000 (60% in capital metropolitan area).
- In 1918 became "sovereign state" under Danish Crown; 1944 Full independence.
- Volcanic island.
- About 79% of Iceland's land area, which is of recent volcanic origin, consists of glaciers, lakes, a mountainous lava desert, and other wasteland.
- Climate is moderate thanks to the Gulf Stream's moderating influence.

- Natural resources: Marine products, hydroelectric and geothermal power.
- Major exports: Aluminum and marine products.
- In 930 A.D., established the oldest parliament in the world.
- Iceland is the only NATO country with no standing military of its own.
- No railroads.
- After 55 years, U.S. Air Force base was closed.
- Hosted 1986 summit between President Regan and Gorbachev.

Based on this information, if Iceland was in the news again, you may see a question similar to this:

Question: The following is an island nation based in a volcanic island formation just south of the Arctic Circle. This country became a sovereign country under the Danish crown in 1918 and later gained independence. It is currently the only member of NATO without a standing army. The population is based on coastal cities that are only connected by roads; no railroads exist in this country. Which of the following is this country?
   (1) Greenland
   (2) Faroe Islands
   (3) Iceland
   (4) Maldives

Answer: If you had read the country profile on Iceland, you would quickly recognize that this is the country that is being described. Greenland is located too far North (not South of the Arctic Circle), the Maldives are in the Indian Ocean. The Faroe Islands are still under the Danish crown. Even if you did not know this, a country you have never heard of (after reading The Economist for 6^{+} months) is unlikely to be the answer.

CIA World Factbook

The CIA World Factbook provides information about different countries. Some of the most helpful items in the Factbook are "Country Comparison" lists. We have included data from some of the lists we consider most relevant to the FSOT, and we will periodically update these lists at our web site: www.FSOTreview.com.

The Factbook lists countries in order of importance along several factors, such as area, population, etc. We focused our lists on trade and natural resources, which we believe are the most relevant to the FSOT. When reading these lists, focus on the order (i.e., who is the largest) rather than on the actual values (e.g., import values). Also, you should also pay attention to the largest regional players (e.g., the largest oil producer in Africa).

Largest Exporters and Importers

Top Exporters (2012)	$ Trillion
1) China	2.1
2) USA	1.6
3) Germany	1.5
4) Japan	0.8
5) France	0.6

Top Importers (2012)	$ Trillion
1) USA	2.4
2) China	1.8
3) Germany	1.3
4) Japan	0.9
5) France	0.7

Largest US Trading Partners

US Exports (2011)	%
1) Canada	19%
2) Mexico	13%
3) China	7%
4) Japan	5%

US Imports (2011)	%
1) China	18%
2) Canada	14%
3) Mexico	12%
4) Japan	6%
5) Germany	4%

You may notice that Canada is the United States' largest trading partner, with 19% of US exports and 14% of US imports. U.S. exports are $1.6 trillion while U.S. Imports are $2.4 trillion.

Crude Oil

Production (2012)	MM bbl/day
1) Russia	10.4
2) Saudi Arabia	10.0
3) USA	9.0
4) Iran	4.2
5) China	4.2
6) Canada	3.6
7) UAE	3.1
8) Mexico	2.9
9) Iraq	2.9
10) Kuwait	2.7
11) Brazil	2.6
12) Nigeria	2.5

Reserves (various)	BB bbl
1) Saudi Arabia	265
2) Venezuela	209
3) Canada	174
4) Iran	151
5) Iraq	143
6) Kuwait	102
7) UAE	98
8) Russia	60
9) Libya	48
10) Nigeria	39
11) Kazakhstan	30
12) Brazil	26

Natural Gas

Production (Various)	Cum (B)
1) Russia	653
2) USA	651
3) Canada	160
4) Iran	146
5) Qatar	117
6) China	108
7) Norway	103
8) Saudi Arabia	99
9) Algeria	85
10) Indonesia	83

Reserves (2012)	CUM (Trillion)
1) Russia	200
2) Iran	113
3) Qatar	98
4) Turkmenistan	93
5) Saudi Arabia	56
6) USA	55
7) UAE	43
8) Venezuela	41
9) Nigeria	40
10) Algeria	35

Energy Exports

Crude Oil (Various)	MM bbl/day		Natural Gas (2010/11)	BB bbl
1) Saudi Arabia	6.9		1) Russia	200
2) Russia	4.7		2) Qatar	113
3) Iraq	2.6		3) Norway	98
4) Iran	2.3		4) Canada	93
5) Nigeria	2.1		5) Algeria	56
6) UAE	2.0		6) Netherlands	55
7) Norway	1.8		7) USA	43
8) Angola	1.8		8) Indonesia	41
9) Venezuela	1.6		9) Bolivia	40
10) Kuwait	1.4		10) Turkmenistan	35
11) Canada	1.4			
12) Mexico	1.3			

Management Section

For the management section, you may need to understand some basic labor laws, such as those dealing with discrimination. Below are a few laws that we believe you should understand. Information is from the Department of Labor and the Equal Employment Opportunity Commission (EEOC). Equal Opportunity employment laws are principally based on the Title VII of the Civil Rights Act of 1964, which established the EEOC and states the following.

Title VII:

"It shall be an unlawful employment practice for an employer:

(1) to fail or refuse to hire or to discharge any individual, or otherwise to discriminate against any individual with respect to his compensation, terms, conditions, or privileges of employment, because of such individual's race, color, religion, sex, or national origin; or

(2) to limit, segregate, or classify employees or applicants for employment in any way which would deprive or tend to deprive any individual of employment opportunities or otherwise adversely affect his status as an employee, because of such individual's race, color, religion, sex, or national origin.

Notwithstanding any other provision of this subchapter, (1) it shall not be an unlawful employment practice for an employer [...] to hire and employ employees on the basis of his religion, sex, or national origin in those certain instances where religion, sex, or national origin is a bona fide occupational qualification reasonably necessary to the normal operation of that particular business or enterprise, and (2) it shall not be an unlawful employment practice for a school, college, university, or other educational institution or institution of learning to hire and employ employees of a particular religion if such school, college, university, or other educational institution or institution of learning is, in whole or in substantial part, owned, supported, controlled, or managed by a particular religion or by a particular religious corporation, association, or society, or if the curriculum of such school, college, university, or other educational institution or institution of learning is directed toward the propagation of a particular religion."

Below is a summary of how some of the EEOC rules and other labor regulations affect companies.

The Family and Medical Leave Act
Administered by the Wage and Hour Division, the Family and Medical Leave Act (FMLA) requires <u>employers of 50 or more employees</u> to give up to <u>12 weeks of unpaid, job-protected leave</u> to eligible employees for the birth or adoption of a child or for the serious illness of the employee or a spouse, child or parent.

Equal Employment Opportunity Commission
The U.S. Equal Employment Opportunity Commission enforces Federal laws prohibiting employment discrimination. These laws protect against employment discrimination when it involves:

- Unfair treatment because of race, color, religion, sex (including pregnancy), national origin, age (40 or older), disability or genetic information.

- Harassment by managers, co-workers, or others in the workplace, because of race, color, religion, sex (including pregnancy), national origin, age (40 or older), disability or genetic information.

- Denial of a reasonable workplace accommodation needed because of religious beliefs or disability.

- Retaliation because one complained about job discrimination, or assisted with a job discrimination investigation or lawsuit.

Employers
An employer must have a certain number of employees to be covered by EEOC laws. This number varies depending on the type of employer (for example, whether the employer is a private company, a state or local government agency, a federal agency, an employment agency, or a labor union) and the kind of discrimination alleged (for example, discrimination based on a person's race, color, religion, sex (including pregnancy), national origin, age (40 or older), disability or genetic information).

<u>15 or more employees</u>: If there is a complaint involving **race, color, religion, sex** (including pregnancy), **national origin, disability or genetic information**, the business is covered by these laws if it has 15 or more employees.

<u>20 or more employees</u>: If there is a complaint involving **age discrimination**, the business is covered by these laws if it has 20 or more employees.

50 or more employees: If there is a complaint involving **family leave**, the business is covered by these laws if it has 50 or more employees

Notice the difference: Age discrimination applies to larger businesses (20 or more employees) than other types of discrimination (15 or more employees). Family leave of 12 weeks only applies to even larger employers with 50 or more employees.

Virtually all employers are covered by the Equal Pay Act (EPA), which makes it illegal to pay different wages to men and women if they perform substantially equal work in the same workplace.

Age Discrimination

Age discrimination involves treating someone (an applicant or employee) less favorably because of his age. The Age Discrimination in Employment Act (ADEA) only forbids age discrimination against people who are age 40 or older. It does not protect workers under the age of 40, although some states do have laws that protect younger workers from age discrimination.

It is not illegal for an employer or other covered entity to favor an older worker over a younger one, even if both workers are age 40 or older.

The law forbids discrimination when it comes to any aspect of employment, including hiring, firing, pay, job assignments, promotions, layoff, training, fringe benefits, and any other term or condition of employment.

It is unlawful to harass a person because of his or her age. Harassment can include, for example, offensive remarks about a person's age. Although the law doesn't prohibit simple teasing, offhand comments, or isolated incidents that aren't very serious, harassment is illegal when it is so frequent or severe that it creates a hostile or offensive work environment or when it results in an adverse employment decision (such as the victim being fired or demoted). The harasser can be the victim's supervisor, a supervisor in another area, a co-worker, or someone who is not an employee of the employer, such as a client or customer.

Disability Discrimination

Disability discrimination occurs when an employer treats a qualified individual with a disability who is an employee or applicant unfavorably because she has a disability.

Disability discrimination also occurs when an employer treats an applicant or employee less favorably because she has a history of a disability (such as cancer that is controlled or in remission) or because she is believed (even if this is not true) to have a physical or mental impairment that is not transitory (lasting or expected to last six months or less) and minor.

The law requires an employer to provide reasonable accommodation to an employee or job applicant with a disability, unless doing so would cause significant difficulty or expense for the employer ("undue hardship"). The law also protects people from discrimination based on their relationship with a person with a disability (even if they do not themselves have a disability). For example, it is illegal to discriminate against an employee because her husband has a disability.

The law forbids discrimination when it comes to any aspect of employment, including hiring, firing, pay, job assignments, promotions, layoff, training, fringe benefits, and any other term or condition of employment.

It is illegal to harass an applicant or employee because he has a disability, had a disability in the past, or is believed to have a physical or mental impairment that is not transitory (lasting or expected to last six months or less) and minor. Harassment can include, for example, offensive remarks about a person's disability. Although the law doesn't prohibit simple teasing, offhand comments, or isolated incidents that aren't very serious, harassment is illegal when it is so frequent or severe that it creates a hostile or offensive work environment or when it results in an adverse employment decision (such as the victim being fired or demoted). The harasser can be the victim's supervisor, a supervisor in another area, a co-worker, or someone who is not an employee of the employer, such as a client or customer.

Disability Discrimination & Reasonable Accommodation

The law requires an employer to provide reasonable accommodation to an employee or job applicant with a disability, unless doing so would cause significant difficulty or expense for the employer. A reasonable accommodation is a change in the work environment (or in the way things are usually done) to help a person with a disability apply for a job, perform the duties of a job, or enjoy the benefits and privileges of employment. Reasonable accommodation might include, for example, making the workplace accessible for wheelchair users or providing a reader or interpreter for someone who is blind or hearing impaired.

While the federal anti-discrimination laws don't require an employer to accommodate an employee who must care for a disabled family member, the Family and Medical Leave Act (FMLA) may require an employer to take such steps.

An employer doesn't have to provide an accommodation if doing so would cause undue hardship to the employer. Undue hardship means that the accommodation would be too difficult or too expensive to provide, in light of the employer's size, financial resources, and the needs of the business. An employer may not refuse to provide an accommodation just because it involves some cost. An employer does not have to provide the exact accommodation the employee or job applicant wants. If more than one accommodation works, the employer may choose which one to provide. If providing a particular accommodation would result in undue hardship, the employer should consider whether another accommodation exists that would not.

Most accommodations are not expensive:
- One-fifth cost nothing.
- More than half of them only cost between $1 and $500.
- The median cost is approximately $240.
- Technological advances continue to reduce the cost of many accommodations.
- Some employees provide their own accommodations in the form of assistive devices or equipment.

Regardless of cost, you do not need to provide an accommodation that would pose significant difficulty in terms of the operation of your business.

Example: A store clerk with a disability asks to work part-time as a reasonable accommodation, which would leave part of one shift staffed by one clerk instead of two. This arrangement poses an undue hardship if it causes untimely customer service.

Example: An employee with a disability asks to change her scheduled arrival time from 9:00 a.m. to 10:00 a.m. to attend physical therapy appointments and to stay an hour later. If this accommodation would not affect her ability to complete work in a timely manner or disrupt service to clients or the performance of other workers, it does not pose an undue hardship.

Example: A grocery store bagger develops a disability that makes her unable to lift any item weighing more than five pounds. The store does not have to grant an accommodation removing its fifteen-pound lifting requirement if doing so would remove the main job duty of placing items into bags and handing filled bags to customers or placing them in grocery carts.

Example: A hotel that requires its housekeepers to clean 16 rooms per day does not have to lower this standard for an employee with a disability.

Example: You do not have to tolerate violence, threats of violence, theft, or destruction of property, even if the employee claims that a disability caused the misconduct.

Definition of Disability
Not everyone with a medical condition is protected by the law. In order to be protected, a person must be qualified for the job and have a disability as defined by the law.

A person can show that he or she has a disability in one of three ways:
- A person may be disabled if he or she has a physical or mental condition that substantially limits a major life activity (such as walking, talking, seeing, hearing, or learning).
- A person may be disabled if he or she has a history of a disability (such as cancer that is in remission).

- A person may be disabled if he has a physical or mental impairment that is not transitory (lasting or expected to last six months or less) and minor.

The law places strict limits on employers when it comes to asking job applicants to answer medical questions, take a medical exam, or identify a disability. For example, an employer may not ask a job applicant to answer medical questions or take a medical exam before extending a job offer. An employer also may not ask job applicants if they have a disability (or about the nature of an obvious disability). An employer may ask job applicants whether they can perform the job and how they would perform the job, with or without a reasonable accommodation.

After a job is offered to an applicant, the law allows an employer to condition the job offer on the applicant answering certain medical questions or successfully passing a medical exam, but only if all new employees in the same type of job have to answer the questions or take the exam. Once a person is hired and has started work, an employer generally can only ask medical questions or require a medical exam if the employer needs medical documentation to support an employee's request for an accommodation or if the employer believes that an employee is not able to perform a job successfully or safely because of a medical condition.

The law also requires that employers keep all medical records and information confidential and in separate medical files.

Equal Pay/Compensation Discrimination
The Equal Pay Act requires that men and women in the same workplace be given equal pay for equal work. The jobs need not be identical, but they must be substantially equal. Job content (not job titles) determines whether jobs are substantially equal. All forms of pay are covered by this law, including salary, overtime pay, bonuses, stock options, profit sharing and bonus plans, life insurance, vacation and holiday pay, cleaning or gasoline allowances, hotel accommodations, reimbursement for travel expenses, and benefits. If there is an inequality in wages between men and women, employers may not reduce the wages of either sex to equalize their pay.

National Origin Discrimination
National origin discrimination involves treating people (applicants or employees) unfavorably because they are from a particular country or part of the world, because of ethnicity or accent, or because they appear to be of a certain ethnic background (even if they are not). National origin discrimination also can involve treating people unfavorably because they are married to (or associated with) a person of a certain national origin or because of their connection with an ethnic organization or group. Discrimination can occur when the victim and the person who inflicted the discrimination are the same national origin.

The law forbids discrimination when it comes to any aspect of employment, including hiring, firing, pay, job assignments, promotions, layoff, training, fringe benefits, and any other term or condition of employment.

It is unlawful to harass a person because of his or her national origin. Harassment can include, for example, offensive or derogatory remarks about a person's national origin, accent or ethnicity. Although the law doesn't prohibit simple teasing, offhand comments, or isolated incidents that are not very serious, harassment is illegal when it is so frequent or severe that it creates a hostile or offensive work environment or when it results in an adverse employment decision (such as the victim being fired or demoted). The harasser can be the victim's supervisor, a supervisor in another area, a co-worker, or someone who is not an employee of the employer, such as a client or customer.

The law makes it illegal for an employer or other covered entity to use an employment policy or practice that applies to everyone, regardless of national origin, if it has a negative impact on people of a certain national origin and is not job-related or necessary to the operation of the business. An employer can only require an employee to speak fluent English if fluency in English is necessary to perform the job effectively. An "English-only rule", which requires employees to speak only English on the job, is only allowed if it is needed to ensure the safe or efficient operation of the employer's business and is put in place for nondiscriminatory reasons. An employer may not base an employment decision on an employee's foreign accent, unless the accent seriously interferes with the employee's job performance.

Religious Discrimination
Religious discrimination involves treating a person (an applicant or employee) unfavorably because of his or her religious beliefs. The law protects not only people who belong to traditional, organized religions, such as Buddhism, Christianity, Hinduism, Islam, and Judaism, but also others who have sincerely held religious, ethical or moral beliefs. Religious discrimination can also involve treating someone differently because that person is married to (or associated with) an individual of a particular religion or because of his or her connection with a religious organization or group.

The law forbids discrimination when it comes to any aspect of employment, including hiring, firing, pay, job assignments, promotions, layoff, training, fringe benefits, and any other term or condition of employment. An employee cannot be forced to participate (or not participate) in a religious activity as a condition of employment.

It is illegal to harass a person because of his or her religion. Harassment can include, for example, offensive remarks about a person's religious beliefs or practices. Although the law doesn't prohibit simple teasing, offhand comments, or isolated incidents that aren't very serious, harassment is illegal when it is so frequent or severe that it creates a hostile or offensive work environment or when it results in an adverse employment decision (such as the victim being fired or demoted). The harasser can be the victim's supervisor, a supervisor in another area, a co-worker, or someone who is not an employee of the employer, such as a client or customer.

Title VII also prohibits workplace or job segregation based on religion (including religious garb and grooming practices), such as assigning an employee to a non-customer contact position because of actual or feared customer preference.

The law requires an employer to reasonably accommodate an employee's religious beliefs or practices, unless doing so would cause more than a minimal burden on the operations of the employer's business. This means an employer may be required to make reasonable adjustments to the work environment that will allow an employee to practice his or her religion. Examples of some common religious accommodations include flexible scheduling, voluntary shift substitutions or swaps, job reassignments, and modifications to workplace policies or practices.

Unless it would be an undue hardship on the employer's operation of its business, an employer must reasonably accommodate an employee's religious beliefs or practices. This applies not only to schedule changes or leave for religious observances, but also to such things as dress or grooming practices that an employee has for religious reasons. These might include, for example, wearing particular head coverings or other religious dress (such as a Jewish yarmulke or a Muslim headscarf), or wearing certain hairstyles or facial hair (such as Rastafarian dreadlocks or Sikh uncut hair and beard). It also includes an employee's observance of a religious prohibition against wearing certain garments (such as pants or miniskirts).

When an employee or applicant needs a dress or grooming accommodation for religious reasons, he should notify the employer that he needs such an accommodation for religious reasons. If the employer reasonably needs more information, the employer and the employee should engage in an interactive process to discuss the request. If it would not pose an undue hardship, the employer must grant the accommodation.

An employer does not have to accommodate an employee's religious beliefs or practices if doing so would cause undue hardship to the employer. An accommodation may cause undue hardship if it is costly, compromises workplace safety, decreases workplace efficiency, infringes on the rights of other employees, or requires other employees to do more than their share of potentially hazardous or burdensome work.

Exceptions
Religious Organization Exception: Religious organizations are permitted to give employment preference to members of their own religion. The exception applies only to those institutions whose "purpose and character are primarily religious." Factors to consider that would indicate whether an entity is religious include: whether its articles of incorporation state a religious purpose; whether its day-to-

day operations are religious (e.g., are the services the entity performs, the product it produces, or the educational curriculum it provides directed toward propagation of the religion?); whether it is not-for-profit; and whether it is affiliated with, or supported by, a church or other religious organization.

This exception is not limited to religious activities of the organization. However, it only allows religious organizations to prefer to employ individuals who share their religion. The exception does not allow religious organizations otherwise to discriminate in employment on the basis of race, color, national origin, sex, age, or disability. Thus, a religious organization is not permitted to engage in racially discriminatory hiring by asserting that a tenet of its religious beliefs is not associating with people of other races.

Ministerial Exception: Courts have held that clergy members generally cannot bring claims under the federal employment discrimination laws, including Title VII, the Age Discrimination in Employment Act, the Equal Pay Act, and the Americans with Disabilities Act. This "ministerial exception" comes not from the text of the statutes, but from the First Amendment principle that governmental regulation of church administration, including the appointment of clergy, impedes the free exercise of religion and constitutes impermissible government entanglement with church authority. The exception applies only to employees who perform essentially religious functions, namely those whose primary duties consist of engaging in church governance, supervising a religious order, or conducting religious ritual, worship, or instruction. Some courts have made an exception for harassment claims where they concluded that analysis of the case would not implicate these constitutional constraints.

Sexual Harassment
It is unlawful to harass a person (an applicant or employee) because of that person's gender. Harassment can include "sexual harassment" or unwelcome sexual advances, requests for sexual favors, and other verbal or physical harassment of a sexual nature.

Harassment does not have to be of a physical nature, however, and can include offensive remarks about a person's gender. For example, it is illegal to harass a woman by making offensive comments about women in general. Both victim and the harasser can be either a woman or a man, and the victim and harasser can be the same sex.

Although the law doesn't prohibit simple teasing, offhand comments, or isolated incidents that are not very serious, harassment is illegal when it is so frequent or severe that it creates a hostile or offensive work environment or when it results in an adverse employment decision (such as the victim being fired or demoted). The harasser can be the victim's supervisor, a supervisor in another area, a co-worker, or someone who is not an employee of the employer, such as a client or customer.

English Expression Test

The English expression usage test is a grammar test similar to the ACT English Test. Since ACT conducts both the ACT exam and the FSOT, the types of questions in these English tests are extremely similar. Thus, Adar Review recommends that you study the English Test preparation materials for the ACT. Amazon offers a number of good preparation materials for prices ranging from $10 to $20, including materials from Princeton Review, McGraw Hill or Kaplan.

We recommend that you take the English expression section of the FSOT Study Guide (available for $29 from ACT at www.act.org/fsot/) under test-like conditions. If you have difficulties with the English Expression section of the FSOT Study Guide, the ACT preparation courses should provide sufficient grammar instruction to properly prepare for the FSOT test. Even if you do well on the practice test in the FSOT Study Guide, it is a good idea to take a couple of ACT English practice tests.

The Adar Review program does not provide practice questions for the English Expression portion of the test because the ACT preparation materials discussed above cover this section of the exam thoroughly.

Biographical Information

The Biographical Information section consists of 75 questions that you must answer in 40 minutes, giving you an average of 32 seconds for each question. Further, this is the only section of the multiple choice portion of the exam that asks you to type examples.

Biographical questions can look like either of these two examples:

| During the last year, how many presentations have you made to groups of 10 or more people?

  A. 0
  B. 1-2
  C. 3-4
  D. More than 4 | During the last year, how many presentations have you made to groups of 10 or more people?

  A. 0
  B. 1-2
  C. 3-4
  D. More than 4

If you answered B, C or D list them (list no more than four)

_____
_____
_____ |

Source: Guide to the Foreign Service Officer Test (www.state.gov)

The Department of State purposefully gives you a very limited time to think about the answers so that you will respond truthfully based on "your first impression". The ACT Study Guide may lead you to believe that the biographical section is less important than the other two sections and that you cannot prepare for it. As we will show in this section, we disagree with ACT's statements that the Biographical Information section "does not consist of questions with right and wrong answers" and that "advance preparation" is not necessary.

Based on a review of web sites, blogs and other sources, we believe that many candidates who did not properly prepare for the Biographical Information section either failed the FSOT or received a low passing score in the test, which may have precluded them from being invited to the Oral Assessment. In 2009 the passing score was 154 points[4]. The Yahoo Group FSWE surveys candidates after the exam and asks them to post their scores on each of the three multiple choice sections of the exam. We looked at passing and non-passing scores and discovered that several people failed the exam despite achieving relatively high scores in the Job Knowledge and English Expression sections of the exam. For example,

---

[4] Source: Yahoo Groups FSWE

one candidate received a score of 61 in the Job Knowledge section and 58 in English Expression (both very good scores), but failed because he received a score of 33 in Biographic Information and his total score was 151, just short of the passing grade of 154.

At the other end of the scale, a candidate received a score of 46 on the Job Knowledge portion of the test and a score of 52 in the English Expression section – significantly below what we would consider a passing grade, but passed the exam because he received a score of 60 on the Biographical Information section. The total score was 158 and the person passed the multiple choice section of the exam.

Right and Wrong Answers
The passing grade for the multiple choice portion of the exam is calculated by adding the points that you receive in each of its three sections: Job Knowledge, English Expression and Biographical Information. Thus, obtaining a good score in the biographical information is necessary to pass the written exam – and since there is a passing score, there must be right and wrong answers.

Advance Preparation
Many candidates complained in forums that the Biographical Information section was much more difficult than they had expected and that they wished they had prepared better. One candidate posted the following comment on the FSWE Yahoo Group: "Biographical was surprisingly hard. […] I had some form of an answer down for every question, but had no time to go back to the questions I had marked for review. […] I could have used an extra […] 5 mins." Similarly, another person writing online stated: "Biographic portion is a killer. I didn't finish the last 10 questions." You will need to prepare before the exam to ensure that you have time to answer all the questions.

The Department of State does not offer any guidance on what you need to do to pass the Biographical Information of the exam, other than to say that **you should answer all the questions** and that you should not lie in order to answer questions the way that you think the Department of State wants you to answer them. Note that if you pass the written exam you will have to take the Oral Assessment (i.e., an interview) in which the interviewer may ask for additional detail on the biographical information you provided. If you lied in the Biographical Information section of the exam, you will likely get caught during the Oral Examination or the subsequent stages of the selection process.

As we mentioned before, many candidates have difficulty answering all 75 questions within the limited time. They may get a lower score than they should if they do not answer all the questions or if they can't think of examples to write. Candidates who fail the FSOT because of the Biographical Information section will have to wait one year before being allowed to retake the test.

Adar Review recommends the following steps to succeed in the Biographical section:
    (1) Review sample questions
    (2) Prepare examples
    (3) Think broadly
    (4) Be confident
    (5) Build your resume
    (6) Answer all the questions

We will base our discussion below on a sample question that asks how many events you have organized that were attended by more than 10 people, and asks you to list a few of them.

Review Sample Questions
There are two official sources of practice questions for the Biographical Section: The Guide to the Foreign Service Officer Test and the ACT Study Guide. The Guide to the Foreign Service Officer Test includes 10 practice questions and is available for free at www.state.gov (you can find link in the Resources/Links page of the Adar Review web site at www.FSOTreview.com). The ACT Study Guide provides an additional 26 examples.

The first step to prepare for the Biographical information is to take these sample tests and answer each question as well as you can. Take as much time as you need to answer these questions. Even though the actual questions in the exam will be different, going through this exercise will help you answer the questions in the exam more quickly.

Prepare Examples
It is very important to think hard about examples for all of these questions. While the actual exam is unlikely to have the same exact questions as the study guides, some of the questions in the actual exam will likely be very similar to the questions in the Study Guide (e.g., the Study Guide may ask you how many books you read in the last 12 months and the actual exam may ask you how many newspapers and magazines you read regularly). You must be prepared to offer short examples to support your answers for all the questions in the Study Guide, even those questions for which the

study guides do not request examples. Be concise, as the software allows only short written responses.

In our example, if one of the questions in the Study Guide asks how many events you organized for 10 or more people during the last 12 months, you should answer the number of events. If the question does not ask you to list examples, you should still write examples as part of your preparation.

<u>Think Broadly</u>
When you are thinking of examples you need to think as broadly as possible. We will explain what we mean by thinking broadly.

In our sample question, do not restrict your examples to work events only (unless you usually prepare events at work). Thinking broadly means that you should think about events outside of work or school. For example, you may have prepared a surprise party for your spouse or a birthday party for your son. You may have organized a dinner for your parents, or a Christmas or Thanksgiving lunch at home. Be creative and think of as many examples as you can well in advance of the exam. Other examples may include a large presentation at work, an event for summer associates, a barbeque at the end of a sports season, your own wedding, etc.

Thinking broadly will help you identify events that you may overlook in the tight timeframe of the exam.
- First, some of these examples may be helpful for other questions that may come up in the exam – i.e., an exam question may ask you about events that you have attended with people different than you (a birthday party with 5-year old children may qualify). Another question may ask you if you volunteered to do something you dislike; a broad answer may include your son's birthday party, where you volunteered to entertain the children to help out your wife.
- Second, practicing thinking broadly about the 36 practice questions in the study guides will help you think broadly in the exam – even if the actual questions in the exam are totally different.

One of the sample questions asks you to list books or magazines you have read about different cultures. A very narrow read of this question may lead you to answer that you only read one such magazine, a National Geographic article about obscure native tribes in Indonesia. A broader view would include people of other countries, languages, races, religions, genders, sexual orientation, other regions of the U.S., etc. This does not only include nonfiction work about other cultures, but may also include a spy novel that takes place in Europe or the Middle East.

You should make as long a list as possible to answer each question. The example above asked you to list books and magazines about other cultures. In your preparation you may want to also list newspapers or books that do not deal with other cultures, but with other things that may be relevant to the foreign service, such as other countries, foreign affairs, East Asia, etc. In the exam you may encounter a question that asks you how many books you have read on either of these topics or in general (such as how many books have you read in the last six months). Having prepared a list of all books, magazines and newspapers before the exam may help you answer any of these questions more quickly during the exam.

Be Confident
Remember that the FSOT is the first stage of a very long job interview. While you may consider that being humble is a virtue, modesty is not helpful in an interview. In the FSOT you are trying to make yourself as attractive as possible to your potential employer (i.e., the assessors at the Department of State). You have to be confident about your skill levels and need to let them know how good you are.

This is very similar to "thinking broadly". The Guide to the FSO Selection Process asks how well you have kept up with the latest developments in technology. Because this question is not written clearly (what does technology mean? What are latest developments? What is keeping up?), two people with the same exact experience may answer it very differently.

- An overly humble answer would be that the candidate has not kept up with developments in technology at all because he cannot program in the latest iPhone app language.
- A more confident person may consider that he has kept up with technology very well because he:
  - read articles about the new Blackberry 10 operating system
  - tried the Microsoft Surface at the local mall
  - reads a couple of articles a week in the Science and Technology section of The Economist
  - read an article about Tesla in the Wall Street Journal

In this particular case, you should not restrict your answers to computers. New developments in oil and gas technology (e.g., fracking) or automobile technology (e.g., plug-in hybrids) also belong in this category. While this is just an example, these recommendations are applicable to a variety of questions that you may encounter in the exam.

As we said before, you should not lie in the Biographical Information section. If you do, you <u>will</u> get caught later in your candidacy. However, this does not mean that you should sell yourself short. You should be aggressive in your answers while being truthful. I believe that the person in the second example above has kept up with new developments in technology pretty well by reading and being informed about it (even if he does not own the latest technology gadget or does not know how to program in any computer languages). If the Department of State wanted to know about your level of proficiency programming in html, they would have asked a specific question about it and not a broad question about technology.

The test may use words such as important, big, feel, difficult, hobbies and technology. While Webster's offers great definitions on each of these words, these words are subject to different interpretations. You should interpret it in a manner that makes you look as attractive as possible. For example, in the example above we interpret technology broadly. Some people may consider that a big event must include at least 200 participants while another person may consider that a home cooked Thanksgiving dinner with 10 people is a large important event.

Build your resume
If you have difficulty answering the 36 practice questions in the study guides, you hopefully started preparing early and have time to "study" for the exam. While you cannot study for the Biographical Section as you would for the Job Knowledge test, you can "build your resume" – i.e., you can gain the experiences that the Department of State considers valuable for your career.

For our original example (organizing events with more than 10 people), you may want to build your resume if you have not organized many events. If your manager is organizing a lunch or an outing for your department, you may want to volunteer to set it up. If your spouse is having a birthday, consider throwing him/her a party. You may also consider volunteering to organize an event for summer associates or for new employees at work or a fundraising event for your children's PTA. This is a way to prepare and gain skills and experiences that the Department of State finds valuable.

There are many sample questions about how you interact with people. For example, one question asks how often you show a personal interest in people at work. This is an important skill in all work environments, and you should start showing a little more interest in people and building your resume. You should also consider engaging in conversation with people of other backgrounds, both at work and in other venues.

The following is a list of sample skills/experiences that the Department of State finds valuable:

- Reading books and newspapers
- Receiving good reviews at work
- Volunteering at work or at organizations
- Giving presentations
- Working in a group environment / showing leadership
- Planning large events
- Taking courses to improve skills
- Traveling abroad
- Attending events in which you know few people
- Speaking to people you don't know
- Interacting with people of different backgrounds/ethnicities

Although you cannot and should not try to change your personality, the following are examples of some activities that you can engage during the six months prior to taking the exam:

- read books (you will read at least 4 books including this one to prepare for the exam)
- engage in volunteer, religious or student organizations, charities and alumni associations; coach a little league team
- attend parties/events
- interact with people of other cultures, ethnicities or racial backgrounds at school, work or at events

If you are interested in the Foreign Service (a given) and you live or work in close proximity to a foreign embassy or consulate, you should consider attending an event hosted by a consulate. Sometimes, embassies, consulates or trade offices host talks, art exhibits or concerts. These offer a good opportunity to learn about the life that members of the foreign service of other countries experience in the U.S., while giving you an opportunity to learn about a different culture.

Answer all the questions

During the exam, you should remember that you need to answer all the questions in the Biographical Information section. Leaving unanswered questions or blank boxes where you must provide examples will hurt your score. When you write answers, be very concise; write like a telegram. You will have a very small space to write your answers and very little time. If you write 4 or more but can only provide three examples, this is not a problem – move on to the next question.

After studying, take the practice Biographical exam at the end of the book.

Preparing for the Exam – Essay

Preparing for the essay portion of the exam is very important. You will be given 30 minutes to:

(1) Read an essay prompt that asks for your opinion on a topic

(2) Decide which position to support (two or more differing views will be presented to you)

(3) Write a 3-5 paragraph essay

(4) Include some examples/supporting arguments

(5) Proof read the essay

Unless you are a very good writer or write often for school or work, this could be the most difficult part of the exam. If you are not used to writing essays often, you should practice diligently prior to the exam.

We recommend that you write several essays within the 30-minute time limit. Afterwards, you should spend more time to proof read and improve the essays further. This will help you think of how you should approach essay writing during the exam.

The important factors to succeed in this section are:

(1) Take some time to think about the question and organize your thoughts (we recommend keeping this to no more than 3-5 minutes).

(2) Organize your essay by first providing a title and short introduction stating your thesis (i.e., your position on the question).
   – Select only one answer/thesis. For example, in a question about assisted suicide, if your thesis is that assisted suicide should be allowed, concentrate your essay on the reasons why it should be allowed – and avoid providing reasons that contradict your thesis.

(3) Provide two or three strong arguments that support your thesis. Include some detailed examples or substantiated details that support your argument.

(4) Provide a concluding paragraph that restates the thesis and elaborates on why you believe this is the correct answer.

(5) You will need to type quickly because you will have 30 minutes to read the question, select your position, structure your essay, write it and proof read it.

(6) Avoid spelling and grammatical mistakes.

(7) Make sure you have a finished essay at the end of the 30 minutes – avoid leaving an unfinished sentence or paragraph because you ran out of time. Although this is not a common mistake, it happens more often than it should.

The computer you will use will have the spelling and grammar check features disabled. It is extremely important that you minimize the number of misspelling and grammatical mistakes because they will negatively affect your score.

The Department of State provides the instructions listed below when writing the essay. Read them carefully now so that you will not need to spend valuable time during the test reading the instructions.

> *"When composing your essay, you should <u>present your point of view</u> clearly and support it. Your writing will be evaluated on the quality of the writing, <u>not the opinions expressed</u>. A successful essay should have an obvious structure and <u>clear thesis</u> supported by relevant <u>substantiating details</u>. It should show your ability to analyze a topic in a way that is appropriate for the intended audience. The writing should be coherent with only occasional lapses that do not impede flow or readers' comprehension. Language should be <u>concise</u> with clear and appropriate word choice. The language should also be <u>free of errors in grammar and syntax</u>, with <u>no more than minor errors</u> in spelling and punctuation. There is no limit on length."*

In an effort to provide you with some guidance on what a 30-minute essay would look like, we asked one of our preparation specialists to write an essay within the 30-minute time limit for you to be able to evaluate what another person in a similar situation would write. You should write an essay on this topic and later compare it to our essay. Take only 30 minutes to write the essay. Start measuring the 30 minutes as soon as you turn the page.

Essay topic

Based on the "Don't Ask, Don't Tell" policy, the U.S. military excludes openly-gay personnel from the armed forces. There are some people who believe that this policy is an egregious form of discrimination that it should be abolished. Other people believe that this policy should be maintained because its repeal would hurt the morale of other soldiers. Yet other people believe that openly gay soldiers should be allowed into the military, but not in combat units. In your view, is the Don't Ask, Don't Tell policy appropriate or should it be modified or repealed? Carefully explain the rationale for your position.

(Do not read the sample essay on the next page until after you have written your own essay.)

An Open and Successful Military

The issue of whether to accept openly homosexual individuals to the military has attracted much discussion in the U.S. and in many other countries with successful military organizations. I believe that repealing the Don't Ask, Don't Tell policy and allowing openly gay people to serve in the military would strengthen our armed services by expanding the pool of candidates and by minimizing stress and distraction for current members of the service that are homosexual.

A military that is open to gay people would have a larger pool of applicants that may bring their skills and capabilities to the service of our country. Many of the concerns that opponents of gays in the military have expressed focus on lower morale among soldiers if gay people are accepted in the military. These concerns are similar to previous concerns about African Americans and women in the military. History has shown both of these concerns to be unfounded. African Americans fought valiantly in segregated units from the time of the Civil War through the Second World War, and they were successfully integrated into regular military units. Women have also served our country's military with distinction, and other countries, such as Israel, have implemented an open policy towards gay members of the military without any negative repercussions.

More importantly, removing the Don't Ask, Don't Tell policy would allow

a significant number of gay and lesbian members of the armed forces to

continue to provide their services in defense of our nation. Since this

policy was enacted in the 1990s, several thousand members of our military

and National Guard have been dismissed from the military. The

immediate repeal of this policy would reduce the number of members that

would be unnecessarily dismissed from our armed forces at a time in

which we are fighting two protracted wars.

An additional problem with the Don't Ask, Don't Tell policy is that it

creates unnecessary stress for our soldiers who, in addition to being subject

to the normal stresses of military life, must also worry about details of their

personal life becoming public. This stress in counterproductive to the

effectiveness of our armed forces and may lead breaches in security. For

example, a soldier based in a foreign country may be blackmailed

regarding his sexual orientation.

The U.S. military can benefit from an open policy towards homosexual

members and candidates. An open policy would make the U.S. military

stronger by increasing the number of potential candidates, reducing the number of unnecessary dismissals, and reducing stress among its members.

It is time to repeal the unnecessary Don't Ask, Don't Tell policy.

Comments on Sample Essay
As you read this essay, it is very easy to understand the view of the writer because the title clearly states that the author favors a repeal of the Don't Ask, Don't Tell policy. We recommend that you add a title to your essay. Although this is not required, a typical college essay would include a title, and so should this essay. Do not spend much time thinking of a catchy title, but make sure that it clearly supports your conclusion.

You may also notice that this essay is on the long side of the 3-5 paragraphs which caused the author to run out of time before proof reading the whole document. You will notice a few obvious mistakes that show that he ran out of time. In the fourth paragraph it says: "This stress ~~in~~ [is] counterproductive to the effectiveness of our armed forces and may lead [to] breaches in security." This sentence is obviously missing a "to" (added in brackets) and misspelled "is". Had the author had an additional 5 minutes, he could have corrected all grammatical errors. This shows you two things: (1) everybody makes small grammatical mistakes due to the time pressure – and small mistakes will not disqualify you; and (2) the longer your essay, the more likely that you will run out of time to proof read it. Although it is unclear how essays are graded, this essay may have received a higher score with four paragraphs and no mistakes, than with five paragraphs.

This essay was written in 2009 when there was much discussion in the press about Don't Ask, Don't Tell, which was a subject during the presidential campaign in 2008. In October 2009 the New York Times published an opinion piece on the subject ("The Damage of Don't Ask Don't Tell). This short opinion piece stated the following arguments in support of its views:

(1) "About 12,500 service members have been forced out, including many with distinguished records or invaluable language and intelligence skills."

(2) "Several other countries, including Australia, Canada, Israel and Britain, have lifted bans on homosexuals serving openly with no adverse effects on military performance or readiness."

(3) "The law has [actually] undermined unit cohesion, in part by […] posing a moral quandary for commanders — look the other way or risk discharging a valuable service member."

(4) "The policy [is] a costly failure because of the lost manpower and the administrative costs of recruiting and separating homosexuals."

Obviously the author of our essay must have read at least one article or op-ed piece about Don't Ask, Don't Tell during this period that provided him with some ideas. Although he did not recall how many soldiers had been dismissed as a result of Don't Ask, Don't Tell, he remembered it was several thousand – this is an important detail or example that supports the argument. It would be much more difficult to write an essay such as this one if one had not read any articles similar to the one described above.

As you can see, it is very important to read about current events. The opinion pages of the New York Times and Wall Street Journal provide some arguments on topics of current interest. When you see topics that generate significant discussion in the news you should read a few opinion pieces with arguments for and against the topic. Some such topics in the news over the last few years include:
- Health Care law
- Assisted Suicide at the time of Dr. Kevorkian's arrest in the late 1990s
- Gay marriage/adoption
- Torture/abuse in Abu Ghraib
- Appropriate punishment for Madoff's financial crimes

The structure of this essay is good, including a title and a clear unambiguous opening statement: "I believe that repealing the Don't Ask, Don't Tell policy [...] would strengthen our armed services by expanding the pool of candidates and by minimizing stress and distraction..."

This opening statement is supported by the three following paragraphs:
- Paragraph 2 supports the statement about expanding the pool of candidates, and attacks the principal argument against allowing gay men to serve in the military – that it would reduce morale. This paragraph also provides two examples of similar invalid arguments made when African American and women joined the military. It also shows that openly gay people are active participants in the military forces of other countries without negative consequences.
- Paragraph 3 states that the Don't Ask, Don't Tell policy caused many qualified soldiers to leave the military. Although this was not part of the opening statement, it also supports the statement about expanding the pool of candidates. This paragraph includes an important numerical example, stating that several thousand members have been dismissed as a result of Don't Ask, Don't Tell.
- Paragraph 4 supports the statement about stress and distraction, and also shows an example regarding possible blackmail.

The essay finally concludes with a closing paragraph restating the thesis from the first paragraph.

Although this is a good essay and the person writing it finished within the 30 minute time limit, the author was not subject to the stress of an exam. Given the time constraints, the essay should have been shorter without losing its impact. Below we have shortened paragraphs 2 and 3 to show what a shorter essay would look like. Note that even if the essay is shorter, the opening and closing paragraphs should both offer a strong statement of your opinion.

An Open and Successful Military

The issue of whether to accept openly homosexual individuals to the military has attracted much discussion in the U.S. and in many other countries with successful military organizations. I believe that repealing the Don't Ask, Don't Tell policy and allowing openly gay people to serve in the military would strengthen our armed services by expanding the pool of candidates and by minimizing stress and distraction for current members of the service that are homosexual.

A military that is open to gay people would have a larger pool of applicants that may bring their skills and capabilities to the service of our country. Many of the concerns that opponents of gays in the military have expressed focus on lower morale among soldiers if gay people are accepted in the military. These concerns are similar to previous concerns about African Americans and women in the military. History has shown

~~both of~~ these concerns to be unfounded. African Americans fought

valiantly in segregated units from the time of the Civil War through the

Second World War, and they were successfully integrated into regular

military units. ~~Women have also served our country's military with~~

~~distinction, and other countries, such as Israel, have implemented an open~~

~~policy towards gay members of the military without any negative~~

~~repercussions.~~

<u>In addition to increasing the pool of candidates,</u> ~~More importantly,~~

removing the Don't Ask, Don't Tell policy would allow a significant

number of gay and lesbian <u>people who currently serve in</u> ~~members of~~ the

armed forces to continue to provide their services in defense of our nation.

Since this policy was enacted in the 1990s, several thousand members of

our military and National Guard have been dismissed from the military.

~~The immediate repeal of this policy would reduce the number of members~~

~~that would be unnecessarily dismissed from our armed forces at a time in~~

~~which we are fighting two protracted wars.~~

An additional problem with the Don't Ask, Don't Tell policy is that it

creates unnecessary stress for our soldiers who, in addition to being subject

to the normal stresses of military life, must also worry about details of their

personal life becoming public. This stress is counterproductive to the

effectiveness of our armed forces and may lead to breaches in security.

For example, a soldier based in a foreign country may be blackmailed regarding his sexual orientation.

The U.S. military can benefit from an open policy towards homosexual members and candidates. An open policy would make the U.S. military stronger by increasing the number of potential candidates, reducing the number of unnecessary dismissals, and reducing stress among its members. It is time to repeal the unnecessary Don't Ask, Don't Tell policy.

Most people have difficulty writing a good essay in 30 minutes. When you first start practicing for the test, you should take longer than 30 minutes to write each practice essay, but with time you should be able to improve in both quality and speed.

An additional and useful exercise would be to write a second essay on a particular topic, but taking the opposite view of the first essay you wrote. This will help you organize your thoughts and make convincing arguments on issues with which you may not agree. This may be useful if at the exam you face an essay for which you do not have strong convictions on either of the possible arguments.

After some time, you should try to complete the practice essays, including proof reading, within 25 minutes (to compensate because you will be more nervous during the exam).

Sources for Practice Essays
You should practice writing as many essays as you can before the exam. There are many sources on the internet for writing argument essays. You may want to try:
http://homeworktips.about.com/od/essaywriting/a/argumenttopics.htm

This web site offers many sample topics such as:
- Is the death penalty effective in reducing violent crime?
- Is torture ever acceptable?

- Should men get paternity leave at work?

Even if some of these topics are unlikely to be in the exam, they are still good examples for you to practice. You can also think of topics that are more likely to come up in the exam when you read newspapers or magazines. One interesting source is:

http://www.economist.com/debate/archive

The Economist's web site has a number of debates that include arguments for and against each topic. You can use these prompts to practice writing an essay and then compare your response to those of the contributors that defend and oppose the thesis. For example, the July 20, 2010 debate was on the topic of gambling and whether it should be legalized. The debate was based on the following opening statement:

> "As with alcohol and drugs, prohibition of gambling is costly and futile. It also makes an ass of the law: because gambling is such a common pastime, enforcement is necessarily selective, and therefore capricious. Yet suspicion of gambling runs deep: Islam forbids it and other religions tend to frown on it. China discourages it, except in Macau. Most Americans oppose legalizing online gambling—despite America's accounting for a plurality (nearly one-fifth) of the $25 billion online-gambling market. Is keeping gambling illegal a reflection of the moral sentiments of most citizens, or is it a waste of resources, a missed opportunity for tax revenue and yet another needless criminalization of a victimless pastime?"

The Economist offers links to articles ("background reading") relating to each of the topics in their debates as well as two essays in support of and against the "house" view. Below we have listed some Economist debates that may be useful for you to practice writing essays.

- Should governments fund the arts? (8/22/2012)
- Have changes made to air travel security been positive or negative? (3/20/2012)
- Should governments subsidize renewable energy? (11/8/2011)
- Is the internet making journalism better or worse? (7/12/2011)
- Will the world be better off without nuclear power generation? (4/6/2011)
- Is the internet inherently a force for democracy? (2/23/2011)
- Will restricting the growth of cities improve quality of life? (1/11/2011)
- Should gay marriage be legal? (1/3/2011)
- Should there be restrictions on gambling? (7/20/2010)

As you read newspapers and magazines on a regular basis to prepare for the Job Knowledge section of the exam, you should think of possible essay topics that you can use to practice. You need to take into account that most of the questions in the exam are more likely to deal with philosophical, social or economic issues than political or military ones. Thus, you are unlikely to find a question on whether the U.S. should leave Afghanistan or whether the U.S. should continue to conduct Predator strikes on Taliban members in Pakistan.

We provide a few examples of essay prompts in Chapter VI.

Chapter III

Foreign Service Oral Assessment
(FSOA)

The FSOA is composed of three sections: Group Exercise, Written Exercise and Structured Interview. This chapter provides recommendations on how to prepare for each of these sections. Please review the sections of Chapter I related to the FSOA.

The FSOA includes three different assessments, a Group Exercise, a Written Exercise and a Structured Interview.

A likely schedule for the FSOA would look as follows:

7:00 AM	Arrive at Assessment Center
7:45 AM - 8:30 AM	Registration and Agenda *You will need to turn in your statement of interest and put all your belongings away.*
9:00 AM - 10:30 AM	Group Exercise
10:30 AM - 10:45 AM	Break
10:45 AM - 12:15 PM	Written Exercise
12:15 PM - 2:15 PM	Break/Lunch *You will likely have 90-120 minutes for lunch. You can use your phone during the break, but remember to turn it off and put it away as soon as you return to the Assessment Center.*
2:15 PM - 3:15 PM	Structured Interview
3:15 PM - 3:45 PM	Break
3:45 PM - 4:45 PM	Exit interviews

You should assume that the assessors are observing you at all times, from your wait downstairs until your final debrief at the end of the day – and should behave professionally throughout, in your exchanges with them and with other candidates. The order of the different sections may vary, but it is very likely that the Group Exercise will be the first part of the exam.

Preparing for the Oral Assessment

You should prepare for the Oral examination just as you would for any other job interview. You should review your resume and important work and school-related activities, as well as your strengths and weaknesses. It is also a good idea to practice doing a mock interview with a friend.

Unlike most job interviews, you have an indication of the questions that will be included in the Oral Assessment. For example, you should be prepared to provide more detail and answer questions about your Personal Narrative. Also, you should keep in mind and be prepared to demonstrate and provide examples of how you master the "13 Dimensions": composure, cultural adaptability, experience and motivation, information integration and analysis, initiative and leadership, judgment, objectivity and integrity, oral communication, planning and organizing, quantitative analysis, resourcefulness, working with others, written communication.

In preparation for the oral assessment, you may want to read portions of the book "Inside a U.S. Embassy: How the Foreign Service Works for America" by Shawn Dorman. You can buy this book for about $15 on Amazon. This book will give you an idea of how an embassy is organized and the responsibilities of the different staff members in the embassy or consulate. This book will help you explain better your reasons for joining the Department of State and to demonstrate that you understand the positive and negative aspects of a career as a Foreign Service Officer.

Important: The Department of State offers preparation sessions to candidates. Make sure you attend one of these sessions. These sessions are very valuable, and the Department of State might check which candidates attended one as a way to gauge interest and commitment. If you attend one of these sessions, dress professionally (i.e., in a suit and tie) and be on time.

After you pass the FSOT and Personal Narratives you will receive an email asking you to register for the Oral Assessment. You may also receive an email asking you to register for an information session. You can also search for these preparation sessions at:
http://careers.state.gov/events/index.html
Choose "FSOA Info Session" from the drop down list to find the closest one to your home. Because there are so few of these sessions, you should participate in one of them even before you register for the test.

The 13 Dimensions
The Oral Assessment exercises evaluate the skills, abilities, and personal qualities deemed essential to the performance of Foreign Service Officers. The Oral Assessment measures your performance exclusively based on the following 13 criteria:

- Composure: To stay calm, poised, and effective in stressful or difficult situations; to think on one's feet, adjusting quickly to changing situations; to maintain self-control.

- Cultural Adaptability: To work and communicate effectively and harmoniously with persons of other cultures, value systems, political beliefs, and economic circumstances; to recognize and respect differences in new and different cultural environments.

- Experience and Motivation: To demonstrate knowledge, skills or other attributes gained from previous experience of relevance to the Foreign Service; to articulate appropriate motivation for joining the Foreign Service.

- <u>Information Integration and Analysis</u>: To absorb and retain complex information drawn from a variety of sources; to draw reasoned conclusions from analysis and synthesis of available information; to evaluate the importance, reliability, and usefulness of information; to remember details of a meeting or event without the benefit of notes.

- <u>Initiative and Leadership</u>: To recognize and assume responsibility for work that needs to be done; to persist in the completion of a task; to influence significantly a group's activity, direction, or opinion; to motivate others to participate in the activity one is leading.

- <u>Judgment</u>: To discern what is appropriate, practical, and realistic in a given situation; to weigh relative merits of competing demands.

- <u>Objectivity and Integrity</u>: To be fair and honest; to avoid deceit, favoritism, and discrimination; to present issues frankly and fully, without injecting subjective bias; to work without letting personal bias prejudice actions.

- <u>Oral Communication</u>: To speak fluently in a concise, grammatically correct, organized, precise, and persuasive manner; to convey nuances of meaning accurately; to use appropriate styles of communication to fit the audience and purpose.

- <u>Planning and Organizing</u>: To prioritize and order tasks effectively, to employ a systematic approach to achieving objectives, to make appropriate use of limited resources.

- <u>Quantitative Analysis</u>: To identify, compile, analyze, and draw correct conclusions from pertinent data; to recognize patterns or trends in numerical data; to perform simple mathematical operations.

- <u>Resourcefulness</u>: To formulate creative alternatives or solutions to resolve problems, to show flexibility in response to unanticipated circumstances.

- <u>Working With Others</u>: To interact in a constructive, cooperative, and harmonious manner; to work effectively as a team player; to establish positive relationships and gain the confidence of others; to use humor as appropriate.

- <u>Written Communication</u>: To write concise, well organized, grammatically correct, effective and persuasive English in a limited amount of time.

- <u>14th Dimension</u>: "Active Listening". While this is not an actual dimension, you should always keep in mind that you need to follow the directions provided by the assessors. Pay attention and do what is requested of you.

Candidates are evaluated solely against these thirteen criteria by four assessors who observe the performance of candidates in a variety of situations designed to enable the candidates to demonstrate the requisite skills. The assessors are experienced Foreign Service Officers from various career tracks. They observe the candidate's performance closely, taking notes during the testing modules. At the end of each exercise, assessors individually enter scores for each candidate into a computer. The average of the scores from all four assessors determines a candidate's overall score. Note that each exercise and each component of each exercise have equal weight[5]. Overall scoring is on a scale from 1 to 7, with 1 representing poor performance and 7 representing outstanding performance. The passing grade is 5.25. In the 2006-07 cycle, only one out of five candidates passed the oral assessment.

Each of the three sections of the Oral Assessment evaluates different dimensions. In general, all sections of the FSOA evaluate: composure, judgment, and your ability to follow directions. You should be aware which dimensions are more important on each section of the FSOA and you should make sure to emphasize your proficiency on each of these dimensions. The following are the principal dimensions evaluated by each of the sections of the FSOA:

- Group Exercise: Oral communications, working with others, initiative and leadership, planning and organization, information integration and analysis, and objectivity and integrity.

- Written Exercise: Written communications, quantitative analysis, information integration and analysis, and resourcefulness.

- Structured Interview: All dimensions with the exception of quantitative analysis and written communications are likely to be evaluated in this section.

You will receive a pass/fail score on the day of the Oral Assessment. After the assessors complete the integration of their scores, candidates are notified whether they have been successful in reaching the cut-off score of 5.25. Along with their final overall score, candidates receive an indication as to whether they reached or exceeded the cut off score on any of the three major components of the exam.

---

[5] The Group Exercise, Structured Interview, and Case Management Study each count for one-third of the total grade. Within the Structured Interview, the Experience and Motivation, Hypothetical and Past Behavior modules (see description of structured Interview below) are equally weighted.

Unsuccessful candidates are informed of their results in a private interview with two assessors. At this point, the candidate is given an opportunity to ask questions about the assessment process and future exams, but assessors are not permitted to provide specific feedback or critiques of the candidate's performance. This prevents any undue advantage to those who take the exam more than once.

Before the Oral Assessment
When you select a date for the Oral Assessment, make sure that you can get a reasonably-priced hotel room for that date. If your assessment center is in Washington DC you need to check for hotels before you select the FSOA date because many organizations have large meetings in Washington that take up most available hotel rooms. You do not want to be in a situation when, after selecting your assessment date, you realize that the closest hotel is several miles away from the assessment center, or that hotel rates are over $300. If your assessment is at Annex 44, we recommend the Holiday Inn Washington Capitol which usually costs about $100-$150. This hotel is in the same city block as the assessment center and you can walk from the hotel to the assessment center through interior corridors without going out into the street. You should check out of the hotel before you go to the assessment center, but you should leave your suitcase with the hotel's porter – rather than carrying it into the assessment center.

Concerning the Oral Assessment:
- Wear a suit. Dress nicely when you travel to Washington. You never know if one of your assessors will see you entering the hotel or walking to the assessment center the previous day (remember to go to the assessment center the day before just to make sure you don't get lost the morning of the FSOA). Have your suit dry cleaned before you travel to Washington.
- Bring a nice pen or mechanical pencil, a neat block of paper and a professional-looking briefcase.
- Bring a digital watch to keep track of time during the Group Exercise and Written Exercise. Make sure to turn off all alarms and chimes before you enter the assessment site.
- The assessors will pay attention to your oral and written communications, but also to your overall appearance and body language. Thus, behave and dress as if you were interviewing with a top-tier law firm or investment bank.
- Valid U.S. state or federal government-issued photo identification.
- Valid U.S. passport or original U.S. birth certificate or certificate of naturalization.

- The Social Security numbers of your dependents.
- All required forms.
- You should also consider bringing an extra shirt, tie and suit just in case you have an accident, like spilling coffee.

See Chapter I for more information.

Group Exercise

The first assessment of the day is the Group Exercise, where a group of 4-6 candidates form a hypothetical Embassy task force charged with allocating resources to competing projects in their host country. The Group Exercise is composed of three sections of approximately 30 minutes each. The three sections are: Preparation, Presentation and Discussion.

The objective of the Group Exercise is to select one project to be fully funded. If there is any money left over, you can decide to partially fund one or more additional projects. You will be evaluated as individuals and as members of a team. As individuals, you will be assessed on how well you analyze the information and present your project. As members of a team, you will be assessed on how well you interact with other members. Remember that this is a team effort and the team needs to reach consensus on which projects to fund – a simple vote at the end in which majority wins is not a good outcome.

Principal dimensions evaluated in this exercise include: composure, information integration and analysis, initiative and leadership, objectivity and integrity, oral communication and working with others.

Other dimensions include: judgment, planning and organizing and quantitative analysis.

After completing the Group Exercise you will likely have a break. Use this time to relax before the next section of the Oral Assessment and avoid second guessing your performance in the Group Exercise.

Preparation Section: Each candidate receives a package of common background materials, as well as a five-page candidate specific project to read and absorb in 30 minutes. At the end of that time, each candidate will present his or her project to the group. Candidates may take notes at any time on a separate piece of paper but you cannot highlight, underline or make notes on the materials provided by the Department of State. You will receive a lot of information to comprehend, analyze and summarize in a very short period of time.

The common materials include:

- General instructions
- Memorandum from a senior US Embassy official appointing the candidate to a task force considering several proposals
- Country Background Notes
- The U.S. Country Plan and Objectives
- Lists of key U.S. Embassy and host government officials
- A map of the country
- Five pages describing your individual project and providing memos with the views of different people from the host country and the U.S.

Critical Success Factors

- Composure: When reading the materials and taking notes, keep the materials organized, keep things in order, and do not look overwhelmed by the amount of materials. The assessors may evaluate your behavior during this stage.

- Planning and organization: Take neat notes and create an organized outline of the presentation. Know which materials are more important (spend more time reading) and which ones are less important (quickly scan most of the country background notes). You will have a very short time to read the information, analyze it, organize a presentation and practice (in your head) giving a 5-6 minute presentation. Thus, you need to prioritize.

- Information Integration and Analysis: You will be evaluated on whether you were able to identify all the important information from the materials provided. If you miss an important benefit or negative of the project, you will lose points. After you identify all the important aspects of the project, you can scan the background notes. If you are able to integrate one or two facts from the background notes you may be able to improve your score.

- 14th Dimension: Follow all directions provided by the assessors. For example:
    - Do not use any information you know from other sources.
    - Only use the information provided in the package.
    - If they ask you to fully fund one project, do not partially fund three projects – with none of them being fully funded.

Recommendations

Read the page on U.S. Country Plan and Objectives carefully. You will need to connect your project to the U.S. interests shown on this page. 30 minutes is a very short time to digest the remaining information and prepare a presentation, so you need to prioritize and spend the majority of this time reviewing your project information rather than general information about the country.

One way of organizing the information is using the "four+one quadrants": Pros, Cons, US Objectives, Costs. This is shown on the table below:

Brief Description of Project: ▪ ▪ ▪	
Benefits: ▪ ▪ ▪	Negatives: ▪ ▪ ▪
U.S. Interests: ▪ ▪ ▪	Cost: ▪ Total cost: ▪ Components: ▪ U.S. vs. other Funding:

Prepare a table like the one shown above.
- Write a short description of your project (what it is, how long it would take, who will do it, etc.).
- Prepare a list of benefits and negatives. You need to be impartial in this phase. Do not minimize (or exclude) any negatives and do not embellish the positives.
- Think in threes: There will usually be three positives and three negative aspects. If you only find two positives and three negative aspects, you probably missed a positive.
  - Although it may sound strange, refer to the benefits of the project and the negative aspects of the project. Try to avoid using the terms "pros" and "cons".
  - Benefits could take any of the following forms:
    - Outright benefits, such as saving lives, educating children, etc.
    - Level of support for the project from embassy staff, other U.S. personnel and local host government officials.
    - Cultural fit with the host country.
  - In a similar way, negative aspects include:
    - Outright negatives, such as pollution created by project.
    - Level of opposition against the project from embassy staff, other U.S. personnel and local host government officials.
    - Lack of cultural fit with the host country.

- When a positive or negative is based on a comment or memo from a particular person, you should attribute the comment (i.e., provide the name and function of the person who made this comment).
- List how the project helps achieve U.S. objectives.
- Cost of project. List the following information:
  - Total cost
  - Cost funded by embassy
  - Cost of different portions/components of the project
  - You may also calculate the percentages (or approximate percentages) for these categories.
- Conclude with a summary
  - Review important aspects, such as U.S. objectives and provide a short Cost-Benefit Analysis (Impact of project compared to amount invested) if possible.
    - Cost Benefit Analysis: Spending $100,000 to provide vaccines that will save the lives of 10,000 children would have a better impact (or bang for the buck) than spending $100,000 to build a school that will provide primary education to 300 children. The first project benefits more people and one could argue that saving a life has more value than teaching a child to read.

Although you should prepare an outline during the preparation phase, you should also try to practice your presentation in your head and check that you will not go over the 6 minute time limit.

Presentation Section: After the preparation section is completed, four assessors will sit in the corners of the room. The assessors do not participate; they only observe the group exercise and take notes. Candidates are briefed on the ground rules and are invited to begin their individual project presentations in any order they choose; however, they are cautioned that projects are not to be compared or evaluated in the presentation phase. Each candidate has six minutes to present his or her project to the others, covering all relevant facts about the project, including both negative and positive points, U.S. interests, and required resources. Time may be left at the end of each presentation for questions from other candidates. In this section of the assessment, successful candidates are able to describe their projects clearly and impartially (including the project description, positive and negative points, impact on U.S. interests and expected costs) within the allotted 6 minutes.

Critical Success Factors

- Oral Communication: Prepare and give a good presentation on your project. Maintain eye contact with the other team participants.

Speak clearly and loudly (but not too loud) – the assessors need to be able to hear and understand you. Project confidence, but not arrogance, when you speak.

- <u>Objectivity and Integrity</u>: During this section, you must provide an impartial presentation about your project. Do not embellish or try to sell your project – and do not lie or hide any negative aspects. If you forget to mention negatives about your project you will lose points on objectivity and integrity – the assessors know all the negatives of each project.

- 14th <u>Dimension</u>: Do not advocate for your project. Do not include any "outside" information. Keep your presentation to 6 minutes. If you exceed the 6 minutes and one of the assessors calls "time", stop speaking immediately – do not say one more word, and do not argue with the assessor. You should also listen and take notes while the other candidates present their projects. Do not practice your own presentation in your head while other candidates give their presentations. You will need to demonstrate an understanding of all the projects during the discussion section.

<u>Recommendations</u>

When the presentation starts, you (as a team) will need to decide who presents first. Volunteering to present first demonstrates initiative and leadership. However, if you don't feel comfortable presenting first, you should not volunteer – do what makes you most comfortable.

You should keep the following in mind during your presentation:
- Make eye contact with the other candidates (but <u>not with the assessors</u>) when you present and also when other candidates present their projects.
- Speak loudly (so that the assessors can hear you, but not so loud that you are screaming or seem impolite to others).
- Speak slowly and clearly.
- Try to present from memory, but if you are unsure of any facts (like the cost figures or the name of a host country official), it is better to read your notes than to make a mistake.
- Make sure you do not exceed the 6-minute limit.
- Be impartial – do not advocate your project.

You should keep the following in mind while the other candidates present their projects:
- Make eye contact with the candidate presenting the project.
- Take notes, including name of project, cost and benefits/negatives.
- Make note of any questions you may have for the discussion section.

- Make sure you understand whether projects can be partially funded. For example, an education project may include the construction of a school and the purchase of books. It may be possible to separate the project and fund only the books or only the school building. A different project may require the purchase of 100,000 vaccines. It may be possible to purchase only 50,000 vaccines for 50% of the cost.

Discussion Section: After the last presentation has been made, the lead examiner informs the group that it is now entering the discussion phase of the exercise, the stage in which the candidates must reach a consensus on project selection and allocation of their limited resources. In this phase candidates discuss and debate the merits and/or drawbacks of the various projects in order to reach a consensus on a recommendation to the Ambassador. Toward that end, the group negotiates and debates benefits and negative aspects of different projects with the goal of reaching a consensus on which projects should be supported and at what level within the allotted 20-25 minutes.

Unlike a job interview where a company seeks to fill an individual position, the Department of State is seeking to fill many positions. While you are competing with other candidates in your group, it is possible for all the candidates in your group to pass the Oral Assessment and it is possible for all of you to fail. You will all benefit by working cooperatively with each other in reaching an agreement. Try to avoid a situation where you are all competing for the attention of the assessors and end up unable to reach an agreement on which project to fund.

Critical Success Factors

- Oral Communication: You will be evaluated on how you speak to others. Be professional. And importantly, make sure you are an active participant in the discussions.

- Working with Others: Be polite, but get your points across. Help the team reach a consensus. Listen when others speak and do not interrupt them. Do not refer to other projects by someone's name (e.g., John's project), but rather by the project's name (e.g., the school project). This will avoid putting people in the defensive. Also, avoid calling your project "my project". You can say "the project I presented", "the project I was assigned" or the "XXX project" (preferred) when referring to your project.

- Initiative and Leadership: This section provides you with the only opportunity to demonstrate your leadership skills in a group setting.

Take advantage of this opportunity, and remember that hogging the conversation does not make you a good leader.

- 14th Dimension: Throughout the discussion phase, you should keep in mind the objective of the exercise: to help the Ambassador decide how best to allocate limited U.S. government resources among a number of worthy projects. Successful candidates have an ability to integrate information not just about their own projects but also about projects presented by their colleagues. They may suggest original ideas and solutions. A good leader can draw out others and help move the group to consensus.

Recommendations
This section has three principal stages: (1) Project advocacy; (2) Discussion; and (3) Consensus.

You will have very little time to reach a consensus. You should use this limited time wisely. Do not waste time arguing about who will go first or who will write the recommendation.

Project Advocacy
At the beginning, you can volunteer to keep track of time (use the stopwatch feature in your digital watch). Even if someone volunteers to be a time keeper, it is important that you also keep track of time. Also, at the beginning the team will need to decide how to proceed. A good start is to ask everyone to give a short summary of their projects – in this stage, you should "sell" or advocate your project. During this stage, you should agree to certain time limits (i.e., maximum of two minutes per person). You may volunteer to keep track of time and stop people when they reach the two minutes. If you stop someone, do it respectfully (i.e., "We have a very limited time and you have reached the 2-minute time limit. Please let the next person speak"). This stage should take 10 minutes.

In this stage, if you believe that your project will not be funded, you can offer additional information about partial funding. For example, you could say how important your school project is for 90 seconds, but finish the last 30 seconds by stating that, while you recommend funding the full project with $350,000, it would be possible to only fund the school books, which would cost $75,000 and would meet three important U.S. objectives: (1) increase exports of U.S. school books; (2) improve the educational achievement of elementary schools in the host country and (3) it would improve local goodwill towards the U.S.

Discussion

During the discussion phase the group needs to work towards a consensus on which project to fully fund and which (if any) other projects to partially fund. This stage should take 10-15 minutes.

The most important part of the discussion phase is that you speak and participate in the discussion. If you are not an active participant, the assessors will not be able to assess you and you will not get a passing score, even if your project is selected.

While you can demonstrate your Oral Communication skills during the presentation phase and the Structured Interview, the discussion phase provides the only opportunity to demonstrate (and not just speak about) your Initiative and Leadership skills and ability to Work with Others.

Initiative and Leadership:

- After each person has provided a summary explaining why their project deserves to be funded, you should start discussing how you will evaluate the projects. You can demonstrate leadership skills by offering recommendations such as: "We should select possible criteria to select a project. I recommend selecting the project that meets the most U.S. interests" or "I recommend selecting the project that provides the highest value for the investment." And then asking: "What do you think?" or "Does anyone have any other suggestions?" to try to get others involved in the discussion.

- Although you should advocate your project, if you believe that another project is more deserving of funding, you can remove your project from consideration by saying something like this: "Although the School project I presented is very important because of: (a) xxxx, (b) yyyyy and (c) zzzzz, I believe that the XXX and YYYY projects are more deserving of the limited funding we have because of xxxx and yyyyy."

- You may also decide to ask each person which project they prefer and why (but nobody can choose the project they presented). After this, you may select to discuss in more detail the two projects that received the most votes. Once you select which project to fully fund, you can continue discussing how to partially fund other projects.

- However, you cannot simply have a vote and select the project with the most votes. This is the discussion phase, not the voting phase, of the Group Exercise.

- You can also show leadership skills by helping to keep the conversation moving in the right direction. Although most of the candidates that make it to the FSOA should be cooperative during the Group Exercise, it is possible that you may encounter an uncooperative candidate that wants to monopolize the conversation. If this happens, you can always say: "We appreciate your views, but we have a limited time and it would be helpful to hear everyone's views. "We haven't had a chance to hear John yet." or "Can we hear John's views now?"

Working with Others:

- You should always be respectful when you speak to other candidates.

- When discussing other candidates' projects, you should not personalize the projects by saying "Peter's project", as this may make people defensive. Instead, you should refer to each project by its most important characteristic, such as "the school funding project".

- As mentioned above in "Initiative and Leadership", if someone is not participating, you should ask for their opinion and try to integrate them into the conversation.

- Do not monopolize the conversation. The Department of State needs to hear all the candidates. If you attend one of the FSOA information sessions you will watch some videos of a sample Group Exercise, in which the Department of State "actors" demonstrate improper behavior. In one of the videos one of the candidates monopolizes the conversation. While many of the candidates watching the video may laugh at the obvious mistakes this candidate is making, the mistakes are common enough that the Department of State decided to make the video. Make sure you find the right balance between being heard and allowing others to be heard. This may be difficult, but you need to try to be seen as polite and respectful to others, while taking a leadership role in the conversation.

Consensus

During the consensus phase you should simply write down the project that the group selected to be fully funded, and the amount of funding for any other projects. There is no need to write a paragraph on funding because you are being evaluated on group dynamics and not on written communications. You only need to write something like this:

> Project X: Fully funded with $XX,000
> Project Y: Partially funded with $YY,000 for books.

You should keep the following in mind during the discussion phase:

- During the group exercise you are not competing against the other four or five candidates in your Group Exercise team for a limited number of positions (i.e., there is no passing threshold, such as only two of the six candidates in the room will pass). In reality, it is possible for all of the candidates in one group to pass, and for none in another group to pass. You should collaborate and do your best in the group exercise without competing unfairly or trying to make the other candidates look bad.

- Active participation is essential. Examiners cannot evaluate qualities they cannot see/hear. Even if a candidate presents the project clearly, he also needs to be involved in the discussion phase to get a passing score in the Group Exercise.

- If the group decision is materially different than what you would have done, you can make your dissention known for the record (and the assessors) – but do not argue or stand in the way of the group finalizing its recommendation. For example, you can state that while you accept the group's decision to fund the penguin conservation project, you believe that the inoculation program for children is more important for X, Y and Z reasons. It is important that you not be argumentative, and to state that you simply want to mention that you disagree with the group decision, but that you do not want to reopen the discussion.

Sample Project

The Department of State provides a sample project for the Group Exercise (FSOA Study Guide available in the Department of State web site or at www.FSOTreview.com). Although the example does not show all the information that you would be provided in the exam, it shows an example of the type of information that you need to include in your presentation.

We have transcribed the information into the four+one quadrants format below to show you how you should organize the information.

Brief Description of Project:	
• Gargon University in the country of Erewhon requests Embassy help in purchasing equipment to complete the university's new sports facility. • The sports facility would include a new pool and a gymnasium.	
Benefits:	**Negative Aspects:**
• The University would purchase U.S. equipment, aiding U.S. business interests and providing good public relations for the U.S. • The Chairman of the Board of the University would be rewarded for being the instrumental force in Erewhon's opposition to a hostile neighboring country's efforts to host the Summer Olympics. • Gargon Regional Rehabilitation Hospital, now sadly under-equipped, would be able to use the pool and gymnasium.	• Gargon is a private university and there is doubt on whether U.S. Government funds should be used to support a private entity. • This grant would not improve economic conditions or raise living standards for the majority of people. • Gargon is the home district of chief opposition leader Reubello, and a grant might displease the Prime Minister.
U.S. Interests:	**Cost:**
• A grant would promote U.S. export trade and support U.S. business interests in Erewhon. • It would enhance public and official perceptions of the United States.	• Total cost: $85,000 • Embassy's cost: $75,000 (88%) • Host government contribution: $10,000 (12%)

You should notice two important facts form this example:

- There are three benefits and three negative aspects. Always search for three positives and three negatives. If you only found two in the materials, keep looking because you may have missed one.
- The Department of State calls the negatives "negative aspects". Not cons, problems, issues or other synonyms – start getting used to saying negative aspects.

There are three things that are not included in this example, but that you should keep in mind when you prepare your presentation.

- If the positives and negatives are based on memos from specific people, include their names and/or positions. Here, only one of the positives is attributed to a person.
- The cost area does not include a cost breakdown of different components of the project. For example, you could separate the costs between the cost of the machinery and the cost of installation or training (if those costs are specified in the project binder).
- Keep in mind cultural issues and show concern for local customs. If your project is to provide family planning in a conservative country, show sensitivity for local customs if they are mentioned in the

materials. Do not minimize local concerns because they do not agree with your political or social views. The group exercise <u>might</u> give you a good opportunity to demonstrate your skill at Cultural Adaptability.

The Department of State issued a new 2013 FSOA Study Guide that includes an additional example of the Group Exercise that is more complete that the Erewhon example. The Kuman example is much more similar to what you are likely to encounter in the exam. However, the Kuman example may make you overconfident. The actual Group Exercise will include significantly more information on the country background and on specific projects, making it more difficult (or time consuming) to sort through the important information.

You can find a direct link to the Department of State' FSOA Study Guide in our site at www.FSOTreview.com.

Structured Interview

The description of the Structured Interview is quoted from the Letter from the Director of Board of Examiners, which you can find in our web site or download from:
http://careers.state.gov/officer/selection-process#nogo

All candidates participate individually in a Structured Interview conducted by two interviewers. For this portion of the Oral Assessment, assessors will have reviewed portions of the candidate's file, including the Application Form, Statement of Interest, and stated career track preference. Candidates are expected to respond to questions based on their personal background, experience, and motivation. This portion of the assessment consists of three testing modules lasting a total of approximately one hour. Each section will last approximately 20 minutes and each section will account for 1/3 of the total score (i.e., none of these sections is more important than the others).

A. Experience and Motivation Interview
In this portion of the assessment, the candidate should convey to the examiners a clear and precise picture of himself, including personality traits, and his understanding of the Foreign Service. The candidate's work experience and <u>motivation to join the Foreign Service, as well as cross-cultural skills are considered</u>. Assessors will evaluate a candidate's potential to serve successfully as a Foreign Service Officer, particularly in the selected career track, by discussing what the candidate has done with the opportunities presented to this point in his life. Candidates must be

succinct and persuasive in responding to the examiner's questions. <u>Candidates should have previously informed themselves about the Foreign Service in general, and also about the work related to the career track they have selected.</u>

This part of the interview is similar to any other job interview. However, you will be facing two interviewers. Make sure that you make eye contact with both of them. When one of them asks you a question, look at the person asking the question. When responding, you should be speak to, and look at, both of them. You should alternate by saying a couple of sentences while looking at the assessor that asked the question and then continue the next few sentences while looking at the second assessor. The assessors will not smile or give you any hint of whether you are doing a good or bad job. They are supposed to be impartial and not to give any indication about your performance (either good or bad) during the interview. Do not be discouraged or concerned by this behavior; answer all questions as best as possible. Do not be worried it the assessors cut your answers short and move to another question. This is normal, as the assessors have a very short time period and the need to cover a large number of questions that address different dimensions.

You will need to be able to express why you would be a good candidate for the Foreign Service (experience) and also why you are interested in the Foreign Service (motivation). Appropriate answers include: sense of duty, interest in foreign affairs, enjoying working with people from different backgrounds, interesting work, helping people form less developed countries, helping people improve their lives. A desire to travel and learn about different places would not be an appropriate response. You should also make sure that these answers are consistent with your statement of interest, which the assessors probably read prior to the interview.

When answering these questions, keep in mind the 13 Dimensions. Try to understand which dimension the assessors are measuring with each question. In your answer, emphasize how you master that dimension and you may also add some additional details that demonstrate another dimension.

Always respond to the question you are asked. If they ask you if you worked during college, respond yes or no, and then add some relevant information, such as listing the jobs you had (if you answered yes) or that you spent your summers and most of your free time practicing for the school's football team (if you answered no). Be concise and always answer the question you are asked.

This portion of the FSOA (and of the Structured Interview) is the most similar to a normal interview. The assessors will ask you about your life experience (school, work, extra-curricular) and why you want to join the Foreign Service. While this may seem like a normal interview, you should still try to focus your answers by highlighting how you master the 13 Dimensions.

How to Prepare
You should review your Personal Narrative and Statement of Interest. You should also prepare by reviewing your professional and educational experience, as well as volunteering and leadership positions, awards you received, experiences living abroad, relationships with foreign nationals, and any other important aspects of your experience. Also, you should be able to explain why you want to be a FSO, why you would be a good FSO and why you want to join your chosen career track.

You should read the books Inside a U.S. Embassy by Shawn Dorman or Career Diplomacy by Harry Kopp. They provide a good background on the work of FSOs and should help you with this part of the interview.

For this section, you may want to practice or read materials about how to prepare for interviews. When answering questions, try to focus on what you did and provide measurable results. Focus on specific actions you took, and explain the outcome of those actions.

B. Hypothetical Scenarios
The second assessment module in the Structured Interview consists of a series of hypothetical scenarios designed to test the candidate's situational judgment. Assessors will either read or provide a document with a brief scenario to read that provides information about a country and the candidate's position in the embassy, setting the scene for the hypothetical situation. This exercise tests the candidate's interpersonal skills, problem-solving abilities, initiative, objectivity, judgment, planning and organizing skills, composure, and cultural adaptability. The problems presented in this exercise are closely related to real-life situations regularly encountered by Foreign Service Officers overseas. This is the only part of the FSOA that can be different for candidates in different career tracks. All other sections are the same regardless of career track.

Although the problems occur in a Foreign Service setting, candidates are not expected to know how an Embassy operates or to be familiar with government rules and regulations. They are asked to fashion a solution that employs good judgment and common sense. The hypothetical scenarios challenge candidates to think quickly. Assessors look for a candidate who can organize for action, take responsibility, and respond to new situations creatively and effectively. While there is no single correct answer, a strong candidate will demonstrate mature thinking, recognize alternative approaches, and consider both the long-term and short-term consequences of responses.

In the hypothetical scenario you will encounter a situation (e.g., you receive a call in the middle of the night telling you that an American was arrested), and the assessors will ask you how you would act. After you respond, they will add information and complexity about the situation (e.g., the person doesn't have a passport or any form of identification). As the assessors add more information, the situation will deteriorate and become progressively more complicated.

In your responses, you should focus on the following:
- Make sure you understand the situation. Think of any additional information you need and who you would ask for such information. In the above example, when you receive the call, you may want to call the local police station holding the American citizen to ask for his name, which hotel or residence he is staying at, and any other relevant information.
- You may also look for any resources that you may need. For example, you could explain to the assessors that you would look for the phone number and contact information for a local English-speaking attorney that other Americans may have used in a similar situation in the past.
- While in real life you can ask a more senior FSO for advice, in the hypothetical scenario you need to show the assessors how you would think about the problem and how you would act. You should avoid answering: "I would ask for advice". While this answer may be appropriate in a difficult situation, , avoid using this more than once.
- State the actions you would take, such as: "I would go to the police station immediately to meet the American person and see if he is in good health and if he needs anything", "I will take the name of a local lawyer to make sure that he can hire legal representation", or "Before going to the police station, I would pack toothpaste, a toothbrush, and some other toiletries."
- Finally, explain who you would communicate with. In this case, you can mention that after visiting the person in jail you will write a memo including the person's name, contact information in the US and other relevant information.

- If you are not sure about what to do (and you are discussing a relatively common situation, such as a missing person), you may say that you would review the Embassy or Department of State protocols for such a situation to understand the proper course of action. It is better not to use this excuse, but to answer the questions to the best of your abilities.

These hypothetical scenarios are similar to case interviews that consulting companies conduct frequently. You may want to read about case interviews in preparation for the hypothetical scenario.

Some key success factors in the hypotheticals include showing that you can take initiative (rather than ask your boss what to do) and also that you can use the resources of the embassy (security, public diplomacy) or other resources (e.g., NGOs) in your responses. For example, if you are asked about a US citizen who is missing in a war area, you may ask the embassy security team for information about how risky that area is and if they know military people in the host nation who could help. Another success factor is to show that you respect your superiors and keep them informed of the situation, your actions, and any outcomes or changes in the situation.

While you do not need to know all the rules of embassy work, you may be able to impress your assessors with an understanding of basic principles on what you can or cannot do in certain situations. For example, you cannot contact a person's family in the US without their consent. Below are a few basic rules you may want to be familiar with prior to your FSOA. You can find additional information at www.State.gov and in Chapter IV of this book.

- Americans have a right to privacy. You cannot disclose any information about anyone without their written permission.
- If an American is arrested, you should go visit him in prison, provide him with information about local lawyers and bring him some toiletries or other items for his convenience.
- You should not pay for bail, but can assist family in the United States who want to pay for bail – such as getting them in touch with a local lawyer.
- You should prepare and submit reports to the appropriate parties.

Appendix A, at the end of this chapter, provides several examples from the Foreign Affairs Manual (available at http://www.state.gov/m/a/dir/regs/fam/index.htm), including sample questions and responses provided by the State Department.

Sample Hypothetical Exercise
(prepared by Department of State:
http://careers.state.gov/uploads/98/f1/98f1f0f4472a93e23bf94b0bde25916
7/3-0-0_FSO_ORalAssessment_April2012.pdf)

You are working in a small embassy in a developing tropical island country. Relations with the United States have been strained for some time, although the island is visited by increasing numbers of American tourists lured by its beautiful beaches, national parks and wildlife, and interesting archaeological sites. The island has experienced numerous tremors recently and ten years ago suffered a major earthquake, which destroyed the port and much of the capital city. You have been at this embassy for almost two years and are looking forward to moving on to your next post. When you first arrived at post, you worked in the consular section, which is responsible for assisting American citizens in distress and for issuing visas to host country nationals wishing to visit the United States. You then rotated for a stint in the management section, responsible for maintenance and upkeep of staff housing. You supervised the local Foreign Service National (FSN) staff charged with maintaining the embassy buildings and grounds. During the past six months you have been working as the ambassador's aide, which required you to move to an apartment three blocks from the embassy.

Question 1: On a Saturday afternoon the communications officer calls you in to the embassy for an urgent incoming telegram that needs immediate action. As you enter the embassy gate, you see two FSNs enter the building. Walking toward the building, you feel a sudden jolt and immediately realize you are in the middle of an earthquake. You have difficulty standing, and see windows in the embassy shatter. Then the earthquake ends. What do you do?

Possible responses: If it appears safe, check if anyone inside the embassy needs help; make sure all embassy employees are accounted for (those in the embassy on Saturday, and those who are at home); check on any American tourists or residents of the country who have registered with the embassy; inform ambassador and Washington about the earthquake; inform and motivate staff to take appropriate actions including finding out how much damage employee residences sustained.

Question 2: After you respond, the assessors provide additional information: The earthquake knocked out electricity all over the city. Because of your in-country experience, the ambassador asks you to lead the embassy's crisis response center. The city's only hospital requests diesel fuel for its emergency generators, which will stop working within 24 hours. The embassy stocks emergency diesel to run its own emergency generators to operate all embassy functions, including communications with the State Department, for three days. What do you do?

Possible responses: Determine exact embassy needs; seek alternative fuel sources; consult colleagues/staff on reducing fuel use; consult host government regarding the hospital's needs; consider establishing limited hours for communication operations; determine when embassy fuel can be replenished.

Question 3: The earthquake hit residential areas hard, and many embassy officers and FSNs lack shelter. Building materials are scarce and the airport is temporarily closed. A local nightclub owner, known for his flashy life-style, offers building materials and labor to the embassy. One of the FSNs reports that the businessman is rumored to be engaged in drug smuggling and strongly urges you to decline this offer. What do you do?

Possible responses: Discuss offer with colleagues; determine facts in case, excluding hearsay; weigh only proven benefits and negative aspects of the offer; seek other sources of supply, including from U.S. embassies in neighboring countries; seek other housing options; contact the U.S. military to determine if they can transport portable housing units or building materials by ship or helicopter.

The Department of State offers a few additional sample hypothetical exercises in the study guide for Foreign Service Specialists. While these examples address different issues what you are likely to encounter at the FSOA, we have added them for your review. The samples below are quoted from the Foreign Service Specialist Oral Assessment Study Guide (May 2013). Some of these examples may include issues that you may see in the Case Management Section.

Question 1: You are the General Services Officer (GSO) at a medium-sized Consulate in a developing country. You depend on the Embassy for most supplies such as office equipment, expendable supplies, and household furnishings. Your requests for supplies meet with indifference and frequent denials. How would you establish better relations with your Embassy counterparts and improve the support for your post?

Question 2: You are the Financial Management Officer (FMO) at a large Embassy. You discover that one of the section heads has purchased expensive coffee table books to give to his contacts as holiday presents. He did not go through the regular procurement procedures and now wants you to reimburse him the several hundred dollars he spent on these books. What do you do?

Question 3: You are the regional Human Resources Officer (HRO) for several posts. One post has never had an employee handbook, another does not follow any standard procedures for hiring new employees, and at a third one local employees threaten to take a "job action" to protest their lack of pay increases for the past three years. Visiting each of these posts requires two days of travel and time on the ground. How would you approach these problems?

Question 4:   You are the OMS in the Management Section of a medium-size embassy. Many of your coworkers come to your boss with requests that they feel have not been addressed by other embassy sections. Some of these coworkers have come to believe that you have influence over your boss's decisions whether to approve their requests and raise their problems with you during social events such as shopping trips or community picnics. How do you respond to these approaches?

C. Past Behavior Interview
In the final segment of the Structured Interview, the assessors ask the candidate a series of questions related to the 13 Dimensions.

This may seem similar to the experience and motivation portion of the Structured Interview. This section allows you to demonstrate how you meet the Department of State's requirements. Before your interview, you should prepare clear examples that demonstrate your ability or your mastery of the following dimensions:
- Planning and organizing
- Working with others
- Cultural adaptability
- Initiative and leadership
- Objectivity and integrity
- Composure
- Oral communication

The Department of State tells you in advance that these are the specific dimensions that will be evaluated in this section, so make sure that you prepare a few examples for each dimension in advance. Hopefully, these examples will be in addition to the examples you provided in the Personal Narrative, or at least offer a more in-depth description than what you provided in the Personal Narrative.

You should try to think of examples from your previous experience that could be used in response to more than one dimension. For example, you could have a very good example in which you work with a group of people (Working with Others) to organize a fundraising party (Planning and Organizing) when you were studying abroad in Paris (Cultural Adaptability). You could use this example as a response to a question from any of these three Dimensions, but try to avoid using the same experience twice to answer two different questions during the Structured Interview.

This portion of the interview focuses on your past experiences, not on hypothetical situations. When you answer the questions, you should do the following:

(1) Explain the situation you faced.

(2) Tell the actions you took. Be specific and focus on what you did. Make sure that your actions support the Dimension being evaluated.

(3) Explain the result of your actions.

It is important to be specific and provide a good background of the situation and description of your actions. As in all other interactions, the assessors will provide minimal feedback. If you do not provide sufficient background and examples of how you demonstrate the Dimension, you will not get a passing score. Before you answer a question, think and organize your thoughts – you can take 15-30 seconds before responding.

When preparing for this section of the FSOA, you should not limit yourself to examples from your work experience. You should think about examples from school, volunteer organizations, hobbies, a semester abroad, etc. Actually, including examples from a variety of experiences could make you appear as a more well-rounded candidate. If you do not have good examples for one of these Dimensions, you can and should "build your resume" prior to the interview. For example, if you are missing some examples of Cultural Adaptability, you can start now. If you speak French, you could join a French cultural group in which you can meet Americans as well as people from French-speaking countries. You could volunteer to tutor children from an underprivileged school. These are but a few examples. You need to make sure that you can demonstrate the 13 Dimensions. If you do not have the requisite experience, you have time to gain some of this experience prior to the interview.

The good news: You have a pretty good idea of what you will be asked: You will be asked to provide examples of how you have demonstrated the seven dimensions listed above. The assessors will provide you a sheet of paper that lists some or all these dimensions. Each of the dimensions will be followed by two questions related to that dimension. The assessors will give you some time for you to think about examples for each of the dimensions and to select one of the two questions for each of the dimensions. The questions will be specific, and the examples you prepare may not work perfectly for all of the questions. For example, you may have one great example about leadership at work, but the question requests an example in which you demonstrated leadership in a volunteer capacity.

It is impossible to be fully prepared to answer all of these questions. Some of the questions will catch you by surprise and you will need to think on your feet during the interview. However, the more you prepare the easier it will be to answer those questions for which you did not prepare an answer.

The following are examples of the types of questions you may encounter. Because questions about one Dimension can be very specific, it helps to have a couple of examples for each of the Dimensions.

- Planning and organizing
  - Provide an example in which you achieved an objective despite limited resources.
  - Provide an example in which you organized an activity for a large group of people.
  - Describe a situation in which you had a very large project to complete and a tight deadline. Explain how you planned to meet the deadline.

- Working with others
  - Describe a situation in which you needed the help of someone who does not work in your department and who had no incentive to help you. How did you get him to help you achieve your objectives?
  - Did you ever have to work in a team with a person you didn't like? How did you manage the relationship? Were you able to achieve your team's objectives?
  - Describe a situation in which you joined a team that included people who did not know you well. How did you gain their confidence?

- Cultural adaptability
  - Provide an example of a situation in which you had to work with persons of other cultures or ethnicities, and tell me how you managed these differences.
  - Were you ever in a situation in which you were working in another country with people who had prejudices about Americans? How did you manage to make them accept you?

- Initiative and leadership
  - Describe a situation in which you volunteered to do something even though it was not your responsibility. Why did you volunteer? How did it go?
  - Describe a situation in which you went beyond what was expected of you.

- ○ Describe a situation when you sought to gain additional knowledge or experience that was not required for your job, but that helped you become better at it.
- ○ Describe a situation in which you demonstrated persistence in the completion of a task.
- ○ Describe a situation in which you had to influence a group of people to agree with your recommendation.
- ○ Describe a situation in which you motivated a group of people to achieve their objectives.

- ▪ Objectivity and integrity
  - ○ Describe a situation in which you had some bias, but remained objective.
  - ○ Describe a situation in which you could have taken personal advantage of someone, but decided not to.
  - ○ Describe a situation in which you were accused of being biased.
  - ○ Describe a situation in which you had to give someone negative feedback. How did you go about presenting issues frankly and fully?

- ▪ Composure
  - ○ Describe a situation in which you were challenged by your supervisor or by executives in your company. How did you defend your views or analysis?
  - ○ Where you ever in an emergency? How did you manage to maintain control of the situation?

- ▪ Oral communication
  - ○ Describe a situation in which you had to present your views/analysis to a large group of people. How did you prepare?
  - ○ Describe a situation in which you had trouble communicating with someone. How did you approach the situation? How did you solve the problem?

When you prepare examples for the Past Behavior Interview, connect each example to as many Dimensions as possible. For example, if the question is about volunteering, you may prepare the following example:

- • I volunteered to manage the summer intern program at work. This is a job that most people avoid because it is a lot of work, and you still have to meet your normal responsibilities.
- • I prepared activities to help the summer interns gain a better understanding of our company, including several presentations by executives from different departments. This was my idea, and it was the first time that summer interns were exposed to company executives.

- I prepared tours and events for the interns to learn more about our city and all it has to offer. Events included a tour of the Federal Reserve bank, a baseball game and a boat ride. I also invited at least 10 full-time employees to each event so that the interns could interact with full-time colleagues outside the work environment.
- I had very limited resources, so I bought the cheaper bleacher seats at a baseball game. Although these were very cheap seats, we had a great time at the game and getting to know each other better. In addition, many of the events I planned (such as the tour of the Federal Reserve) were free.
- Two of the 10 interns were international students from India and Brazil. I had a particularly close relationship with the intern from India. I had never worked with anyone from India before, and I learned XXXX, XXXX and XXXX from him. During the summer they also gained a better understanding of the work environment in the U.S.
- Results: The summer was very successful and all but one of the interns who received offers to join us after completion of their education joined us the next year. The following year, the person who managed the program asked me for help to set up events. The executive presentations became a standard feature of future summer programs.

This example can be customized to answer questions related to four different dimensions:
- Initiative and Leadership: Volunteered to manage the summer program.
- Planning and Organizing: Prepared events; worked with limited budget.
- Cultural adaptability: Two international students; learned about culture in India.
- Working with Others: Coordinate with executives for speeches.

You need to be careful to gain the best use out of each sample experience because you will likely only be able to use it once (i.e., you should try to avoid using the same story to answer a question about initiative and leadership and another question about planning and organizing). I would use the summer internship example to answer a question about initiative and leadership, such as: Describe a situation in which you volunteered to do something even though it was not your responsibility.

I would focus the answer on my volunteering for the activity, but I would also provide the assessors with clear examples of planning and organizing and working with others. This would allow the assessors to give you some extra credit for these other Dimensions. I would leave out the example about the international students. You can use this for a question on cultural adaptability, where you can start with… "During the summer intern program I described earlier, two of the interns were international students from India and Brazil…" and then continue with a powerful example of cultural adaptability.

Although the following Dimensions were not listed as being tested during the Past Behavior Interview, they may be tested in future years. You should also think of some examples that demonstrate your skill in some of these dimensions.

- <u>Information Integration and Analysis</u>: To absorb and retain complex information drawn from a variety of sources; to draw reasoned conclusions from analysis and synthesis of available information; to evaluate the importance, reliability, and usefulness of information; to remember details of a meeting or event without the benefit of notes.

- <u>Judgment</u>: To discern what is appropriate, practical, and realistic in a given situation; to weigh relative merits of competing demands.

- <u>Quantitative Analysis</u>: To identify, compile, analyze, and draw correct conclusions from pertinent data; to recognize patterns or trends in numerical data; to perform simple mathematical operations.

- <u>Resourcefulness</u>: To formulate creative alternatives or solutions to resolve problems, to show flexibility in response to unanticipated circumstances.

- <u>Written Communication</u>: Will likely only be tested in the written exercise.

- <u>Experience and Motivation</u>: Will likely only be tested in the experience and motivation section of the Structured Interview.

At the end of the interview, such as you would expect on any job interview, the assessors will likely ask you if you have any questions about the FSOA or the job, or whether there is anything else that is important that you would like them to know about. You should probably be prepared to answer either of these questions, and to thank your assessors and say something nice about the day's experience.

Case Management Writing Exercise

The final section of the oral assessment is the 90-minute Case Management Exercise. The purpose of this segment is to evaluate the candidate's management skills, interpersonal skills and quantitative ability. Writing concise, correct, and persuasive English is also important in this exercise. This exercise is indicative of the candidate's ability to integrate and analyze information, to interpret quantitative data, and to display sound judgment. The candidate will be asked to incorporate data and other statistical information in the analysis and recommended solutions. *(source: Department of State)*

Unlike the essay section of the FSOT (where the instructions indicate that "Your writing will be evaluated on the quality of the writing, not the opinions expressed"), your opinions and rationale are extremely important in the Case Management exercise. But the way you write and organize your thoughts is also very important. Note that the case management writing exercise is the same for all candidates, regardless of career track. Thus, this section is more likely to focus on managerial or consular issues rather than economic or political ones (see example in next page).

In this part of the FSOA, the candidate is given a memo describing an assignment and several pages of background information, including a summary of the major issues, an organizational chart, e-mail messages from a host of different perspectives at different levels in the Embassy and details about the past performance of the staff. A calculator is not allowed, but the analysis and recommendations will require you to analyze numerical information. This is the only part of the FSOA in which you will be asked to demonstrate (and not simply describe) your skills on the Quantitative Analysis dimension. You need to make sure to include some of the numbers provided within your memo.

The instructions will likely say that you should spend 30 minutes reading and analyzing the material, 45 minutes writing the required memo, and 15 minutes reviewing and revising. Take this advice seriously. Do not take too long to read the materials or you will not be able to finish the memo within the allotted 90 minutes. Time management is critical for success in this section. The 90 minutes will pass by very quickly, and you will be faced with a large amount of information that you will need to assimilate before writing the memo. Many candidates consider this the most difficult section of the FSOA – not because of the complexity of the situation, but because of the limited time to answer the case.

Keep track of time on your watch to make sure that you do not exceed the recommended time for each of the portions of the assignment (reading, writing and reviewing). The memo will be typed on a computer, but as with the essay in the written FSOT, the spelling, grammar and calculator features are likely to be disabled, and you will not be able to write notes or underline on the documents you are provided. As with the FSOT essay, make sure that you do not end up with a partial sentence or paragraph when the assessors call the end of the 90 minutes.

The instructions are very important. Read them carefully and make sure you follow them. For example, if the instructions say to write a two-page memo, do not write two pages and three lines.

Because you will receive a large number of memos and supporting information, a critical skill will be separating between the documents that provide valuable information and those that do not. Within the valuable documents, you will need to separate between data that is necessary for your assignment and data that is not relevant. Also, keep in mind that emails from individuals may contain subjective or incorrect information (e.g., in the example below, Peter may be more interested in getting paid for overtime than in solving the needs of the American staff at the embassy). Pay extra attention to any documents that include numbers, and try to incorporate them into your memo.

Sample Exercise
Prepared by Department of State (2009 Letter from the Director of Board of Examiners), and available as a link at www.FSOTreview.com.

You are the newly arrived Supervisory General Services Officer at a medium-sized embassy in a country with few amenities. General Services Officers are responsible for the embassy's logistics operations: leasing, maintenance, transportation, procurement, management and inventory of property, and the like.

Your supervisor, the Management Officer, Steve Hansen, is out of the office, and has left you a memorandum, indicating that a file on the top of your desk should be your number one priority. His memorandum indicates that a conflict has developed between your deputy, Sharon Smith, who has recently arrived on her first tour, and the Junior Officer in the consular section, Mitch Stevens. The maintenance chief, Peter, a local national who reports to Sharon, is also involved. There are no other American personnel in the section; Sharon is responsible for leasing, maintenance, and property inventories, while you are responsible for procurement, transportation, and overall management of the section. The Management Officer instructs you to draft for his consideration a <u>two-page memo</u> that <u>presents the facts</u> and offers <u>recommendations</u> on how to resolve the issue, including <u>at least one alternative</u>.

Keep the following instructions in mind when you write your memo (underlined above):

(1) Format needs to be as a memo. If there are any memos in the package you receive, you should copy the formatting they use, such as "To", "From", "Date", and any other information they include on the top.

(2) It cannot exceed two pages

(3) It must include a description of the situation/facts and recommendations for actions

(4) It must include at least one alternative

If you write a great memo that does not include an alternative recommendation, you are unlikely to pass this section.

You review the file in front of you. It contains:

- An exchange of e-mails between Sharon and Mitch.
  - Mitch complains that the work orders for repairs at his residence are not being completed to his satisfaction; he has received no follow-up information.
  - Sharon responds that many of his requests are not appropriate use of the embassy's limited maintenance staff.
  - Mitch responds that this was never a problem under Sharon's predecessor, and furthermore, that he himself, as a General Services Officer on his previous tour, allowed such practices and certainly knows the regulations at least as well as Sharon.
  - She in turn retorts that Mitch's personal friendship with her predecessor resulted in favoritism that should never have happened in the first place.
  - Mitch in turn alleges that Sharon must bear a personal grudge against him, apparently because he was recently tenured, while she was not.

- A memorandum from Mitch's supervisor to the Management Officer (your supervisor), complaining that the maintenance section's failure to handle Mitch's household repairs is having an unsatisfactory effect on his work in the Consular Section, and referring to an incident the previous Friday evening at the Marine House, in which Sharon and Mitch apparently resorted to name-calling after a few beers. The Consular Officer also suggests that, since Sharon's arrival, embassy morale has suffered considerably; she is known as "the lady who can only say 'no.'"

- Mitch's work orders, as follows:
    - Repair torn window-screen in kitchen. Marked "Low Priority" by Sharon, with the notation that this is the third time in two years that this particular screen has been torn and is in need of replacement.
    - Repair motorcycle. Marked "Not approved" by Sharon, with the notation that this is Mitch's personal property and should not be repaired using U.S. Government funds or personnel.
    - Build tool shed in back yard. Marked "Not approved" by Sharon, with the notation that there is ample space for tools in the garage, but this space is being used by Mitch's two motorcycles instead.
    - Replace draperies throughout the house. Marked "Defer" by Sharon, with the notation that the draperies were all changed upon Mitch's arrival eighteen months ago, and that they are changed only once per occupant, regardless of the circumstances.
    - Replace living room carpet. Marked "Approved" by Sharon, with the notation that carpet cannot be purchased at the present time because the embassy has no funds for the procurement of furniture and furnishings.

- A memorandum from Peter, the local maintenance chief, to Sharon, cc: Steve (your supervisor), indicating his discomfort with Sharon's new policy of disapproving so many work orders. He says he has been with the embassy for 15 years, and has always provided quality and courteous service to the American staff, at both their homes and offices, and indicates he has a large, able staff of workmen ready to be of service. He is concerned about the effect that the new policy is having on embassy morale, and in particular on the relations between his section and the American staff.

- A memorandum from the budget chief to Sharon, cc: Steve (your supervisor), indicating that, barely halfway through the fiscal year, the General Services Section is considerably over-budget. A line-by-line tally is attached. Costs are all in U.S. dollars.

Activity	Annual Budget	Expended to Date	Remaining
Local Salaries	$450,000	$230,000	$220,000
Overtime	10,000	95,000	(85,000)
Benefits	100,000	52,000	48,000
Awards	8,000	10,000	(2,000)
Supplies	500,000	355,000	145,000
Utilities	675,000	455,000	225,000
Furniture and Furnishings	250,000	200,000	50,000
Equipment	75,000	95,000	(20,000)
Travel	5,000	5,000	0
Transportation	100,000	85,000	15,000
Fuel	145,000	100,000	45,000

- A statistical summary of work orders for past month, as follows:

Date	Requestor	Work Requested	Status
3/16	Stevens	Repair torn screen	Deferred
3/19	Johnson	Repair air conditioning	Completed
3/19	Berman	Paint kitchen	Scheduled
3/20	Jones	Replace stove	Deferred
3/21	Stevens	Repair motorcycle	Not approved
3/22	Cass	Repair refrigerator	Completed
3/23	Stevens	Build tool shed	Not approved
3/29	Haskell	Fix drain	Completed
3/30	Stevens	Replace draperies	Deferred
4/1	Echeverria	Pest control (ants)	Scheduled
4/2	Hadley	Repair air conditioning	Completed
4/2	Haskell	Fix drain (again)	Completed
4/3	Stevens	Replace living room carpet	Approved
4/3	Sanchez	Repair air conditioning	Scheduled

Approved/Completed: 5 (36%)
Approved/Scheduled: 3 (21%)
Approved/Not Scheduled: 1 (7%)
Approved/Deferred: 3 (21%)
Not Approved: 2 (14%)

Questions and Possible Responses[6]

(a) Summarize the situation
Sharon feels that Mitch's requests are frivolous. His friendship with her predecessor allowed his every wish to be granted (causing severe cost overruns in the section's overtime and supply budgets), and –his previous tour as a General Services Officer aside– he now needs a reality check. Mitch, in turn, feels Sharon is being dismissive of requests that are legitimate in the local hardship environment, inconsistent with past precedent, and disrespectful of his own self-acknowledged expertise in her area. Mitch's requests constitute a third of all those made in the past month, and 100% of those not approved.

Mitch's requests are not critical, even in a hardship environment; he has probably been getting by with more than he deserved because of his close friendship with Sharon's predecessor. At the same time, Sharon appears to be too rigid and, perhaps, has failed to communicate to Mitch the justifiable reasons for her actions. Her actions are having a serious effect on morale, not only according to Mitch but also according to other (perhaps more objective) observers. She needs to understand that following regulations and giving good service are not mutually exclusive.

An analysis of the budget reveals that, although the fiscal year is only halfway over, we have already spent almost 75% of the annual budget – and the Budget Chief is concerned about the level of spending at the Embassy. Several budget categories have less than 25% of their annual allocation remaining: overtime, awards, furniture and furnishings, equipment, travel and transportation.

Note: You should use the numbers shown in the tables. Converting dollar amounts into percentages could be useful. For example, you could add the total budget for the year and the amounts spent to date and say that the Embassy has spent 73% of its budget during the first six months of the year.

(b) How do you propose to resolve the situation?
You should notice that there are two issues here: First, an issue between Mitch and Sharon. Second, an issue with the budget and the local staff's probable abuse of overtime pay. While you should focus on the principal question (i.e., Mitch and Sharon), you should mention the budget issue and propose a solution.

---

[6] These questions were provided by the Department of State. We provided some additional comments, notes and recommendations in the responses.

Recommendation: Meet separately with Mitch and Sharon and then meet with them together to determine what can and should be done to address Mitch's work orders. Perhaps the three of you could visit Mitch's house to find practical ways in which he can better help himself where the embassy can't help him. Work out with Sharon a system by which all employees submitting work orders receive prompt communication on the status of their requests, including reasons for their refusal or deferment. Suggest a pro-active notice to American employees on what maintenance actions the embassy is responsible for, and for which it is not, and the anticipated time delays in completing work orders.

In the recommendation section, you should also volunteer to take the actions being recommended (i.e., show initiative). Do not simply say that the Embassy should send a memo to all employees explaining the Embassy policies on maintenance. Rather, you should say that if Steve is in agreement, you will prepare a memo addressed to all Embassy staff explaining (or summarizing) the policy for his review.

Alternative Recommendation: Consider the division of duties between Sharon and yourself; perhaps you'd like to swap the maintenance and transportation functions, so you can get a better idea on how the maintenance section is being utilized.

Related Issue: To deal with the budget problem, recommend an immediate moratorium on overtime, and furniture and equipment purchases; do not fill any vacant positions unless absolutely necessary; look at ways to conserve energy. While not part of the question, overtime is a significant issue that needs to be addressed. You may recommend a review to understand how the Embassy has spent so much of its budget during the first six months of the year, and try to understand if this is appropriate for some expense categories (e.g., at this Embassy, 50% of the travel usually takes place during the first three months of the year) but not for other categories (e.g., overtime).

Recommendations
You should consider starting your memo with a short introduction that is relevant to the situation. In this example you are told that you just arrived to the post and that your supervisor is out of the office, but it is unclear if he is sick, traveling in country or on vacations in the US). You should start the memo saying that you are enjoying your new position and look forward to meeting him upon his return to the office. You can end the memo by saying that you look forward to discussing the next steps with him when he returns.

As always, make sure to follow the instructions; do not make assumptions that are not clear from the instructions. Be as complete as possible in the time allotted. This essay is intended not only to test your management and quantitative skills, but also your written communication ability. Pay as much attention to how you write as to what you say.

The Department of State indicates that you need no previous experience with the management of a foreign post. However, this example suggests that some understanding of basic Foreign Service management may be useful. The Department of State web site has a link to the Foreign Service manual (http://www.state.gov/m/a/dir/regs/index.htm), which you may wish to read or scan prior to the FSOA. Although this may be helpful for the Case Management exercise, it is extremely long and not necessary for the exam. The section on Residences (15 FAM 720) deals with some of the issues in the "Sharon and Mitch" case we just reviewed.

The Department of State uploaded a new FSOA Study Guide in 2013 that includes an additional Case Management sample exercise. The new example is more similar to what you will experience at the FSOA. However, the case in the actual exam will have many more pages and will likely be a little more complex. You can download the new FSOA Study Guide at http://careers.state.gov/officer/selection-process#nogo or at www.FSOTreview.com.

FSOA: Last Steps

Before moving on to the last steps, we want to provide you with one important piece of advice that applies to all sections of the FSOA: Do not be discouraged if you make a mistake, even a big one, but always be courteous and respectful in apologizing.

Real-life example: A candidate made two substantial mistakes, yet passed all three sections of the FSOA and was offered a place in a junior officer class. First, he ran over the 6-minute limit in the presentation stage of the group exercise. Second, he forgot to remove his cell phone after returning from lunch, and the cell phone rang during the Structured Interview. Either of these two mistakes could completely derail a candidacy if the candidate reacts inappropriately, but the damage can be limited (although probably not eliminated) if one acts respectfully. For example, if one of the assessors tells you that the 6 minutes are up, stop speaking mid-sentence – do not try to finish your thought, and more importantly, do not argue with the assessor. In the case of a phone or watch ringing, apologize and immediately turn off the phone or watch. Do not answer the phone under any circumstance.

Similar situations may include arriving late, missing some forms, getting lost during lunch and returning late, missing a suit because you lost your luggage at the airport. In any of these situations, explain the problem succinctly and apologize respectfully. Of course, it is always better to avoid any of these situations by planning appropriately.

After all three exercises are completed, all candidates will go to the room where the Case Management exercise took place and will wait to receive their score on the FSOA. The assessors will come into the room and call one candidate at a time. You may be in this room for an hour or longer, and the wait can be very nerve-racking. Try to remain composed during this waiting period.

Each candidate will meet with one or two assessors who will provide a letter with the candidate's score and additional information. If the candidate did not pass the FSOA, the assessors will explain that the candidate can take the FSOT and FSOA again. If the candidate passed the FSOA, the assessors will explain the next steps, and allow the candidate to ask any questions. They will also give you a letter showing your total score and whether you passed each of the three sections. After this meeting, you will proceed to meet with security personnel who will take your finger prints and start the security background check. At this time you will need all the forms that you were asked to bring to the exam, such as the form SF-86, and your passport. You will also receive a CD-ROM or DVD with additional information about the next steps and how to start the medical examination for you and for family members who would travel with you.

Appendix A: Hypothetical Scenarios from the Foreign Affairs Manual

As you can see, many of these hypotheticals have more than one question. The subsequent questions add an additional level of complexity similar to what you may encounter during the Hypothetical Scenarios section of the Structured Interview. We believe that these questions, while very different from those in the assessment, provide a helpful understanding of Department of State procedures and the type of work to which Consular Officers would be exposed.

PRIVACY ACT EXERCISES

Scenario 1. A U.S. citizen is a victim of a crime in your consular district but does not report the crime to the police and asks that you do not do so either.

Questions
A. Consistent with the Privacy Act, can you report the crime?
B. If so, should you report the crime?
C. The victim's attorney contacts you for information. Can you discuss the case with the attorney without obtaining a Privacy Act release from the victim?

Scenario 2. You are contacted by host country immigration authorities who ask that you confirm that a particular person (not an arrestee) who asserts he is a U.S. citizen is in fact a U.S. citizen.

Questions
A. Can you, consistent with the Privacy Act, reply?
B. If so, should you?

Scenario 3. A U.S. citizen dies in your consular district and his remains are shipped back to the United States. While the remains are in transit to the United States, you get a phone call from the funeral director in the hometown saying he misplaced the contact information relating to the next-of-kin and asks that you provide it.

Questions
A. Can you?
B. If so, should you?

Scenario 4. Waiting at your post when you arrive one morning is a 15-year old U.S. citizen (minor) who wants your help. He confides that he has run away from home. He wants to go back to the United States (and has sufficient funds) but wants your help in arranging travel. He wants to "slip back" into the United States without telling his parents though he "promises" he will contact them when he gets back.

Questions
A. Should you comply with the minor's request?
B. What if he says, "Don't tell my parents that I've been traveling with my girlfriend." Can/should you comply?

Scenario 5. The host government is on the phone. They have picked up a person bearing a U.S. passport and they suspect photo substitution in the passport. They are asking you to provide information about whether the passport number can be verified and whether it was reported lost or stolen. You check PIERS and CLASP and those automated records confirm the issuance of the passport and the fact that the person to whom it was issued reported it stolen. (This example may be way too complicated for a hypothetical scenario, but it is still valuable in understanding the work that Consular Officers do).

Questions
A. Should you confirm that the passport was issued and reported stolen?
B. Should you request a written (faxed) request from the host government and then confirm that the passport was issued and reported stolen?
C. Should you request a written (faxed) request from the host government and then direct the inquiry to the Department?

PRIVACY ACT SOLUTIONS

Scenario 1: A U.S. citizen is a victim of a crime in your consular district but does not report the crime to the police and asks that you do not do so either.

A. Can you report the crime? The Department's Prefatory Statement of Routine Uses provides that this kind of information "may be referred" to the local, state, federal or foreign law enforcement agency charged with investigating such crimes.

B. Should you report the crime? This is largely a judgment call, which probably should involve consultations with supervisory personnel. It would depend, for example, on whether the crime was serious or violent in nature, whether it was likely to be repeated or perpetrated on others, and whether it was part of a pattern that ought to be brought to the attention of authorities.

C. Can you discuss the case with the attorney without obtaining a Privacy Act release from the victim? The Department of State provides that routine use includes release of information to "Attorneys when the individual to whom the information pertains is the client of the attorney making the request, when the attorney is acting on behalf of some other individual to whom access is authorized under these rules." It has been our practice to accept as sufficient an attorney's statement on letterhead that he or she "represents" the person or that he or she is the person's attorney of record. We **do not** require a special form, or separate writing signed by the client.

ANALYSIS:
The first option in such a case, however, would almost certainly be to urge the person who was victimized by the crime to report it directly to the appropriate authorities explaining why it would be important to do so. Only after the individual declined to do so, and after discussions with supervisory personnel, would the consular officer act independently to advise the authorities. Even then, however, the person involved should be informed of the intention to advise authorities. Consult *CA/OCS/L*.

Scenario 2: You are contacted by host country immigration authorities who ask that you confirm that a particular person (not an arrestee) who asserts he is a U.S. citizen is in fact a U.S. citizen.

A. Can you reply? You may confirm the U.S. citizenship of the individual provided the request is made in connection with a determination of a "right" or "benefit" of the individual, e.g., whether the individual is admissible or eligible to stay in the host country. You can also release the information to permit such governments to fulfill passport control and immigration duties.

B. Should you reply? It should be remembered that all releases of information under the Privacy Act are permissive, not mandatory. If there was reason to be concerned about the motive or purposes of the foreign government, e.g., to locate and detain political dissenters, the information need not be provided or, at the very least, inquiry can and should be made as to the reason for which the information is sought.

Scenario 3: A U.S. citizen dies in your consular district and his remains are shipped back to the United States. While the remains are in transit to the United States, you get a phone call from the funeral director in the hometown saying he misplaced the contact information relating to the next-of-kin and asks that you provide it.

A. Can you provide information? Yes, you may provide the information. Information retrieved from the decedent's records is not subject to Privacy

Act protection. It may not be protected if there is not a file in the name (or under some other identifier) of the next of kin, but even if it is, there is a routine use for Overseas Citizens Records for disclosures to "funeral homes in connection with the death abroad of citizens of the United States." You should provide the information unless you have reason to believe that the caller has not already been hired by the next-of-kin.

B. Should you provide the information? Yes, of course.

Scenario 4: Waiting at your post when you arrive one morning is a 15-year old U.S. citizen (minor) who wants your help. He confides that he has run away from home. He wants to go back to the United States (and has sufficient funds) but wants your help in arranging travel. He wants to "slip back" into the United States without telling his parents though he "promises" he will contact them when he gets back.

A. Can you comply with the minor's request? Cases involving minors can present some difficulties, in part, because "the law" (primarily court decisions) continues to evolve in this area. In general, however, the younger a minor, the more information can and should be disclosed to a parent. In the example above, the parents may be very worried about their child and, at the very least, they should be contacted immediately to be assured that the minor has been located and is safe. Moreover, they may well have filed a missing person report with local police who may be diligently searching "in all the wrong places." Again, in such a case the first option would be to strongly encourage the minor to contact his parents offering to facilitate the call, and perhaps, confirming yourself that the information has been conveyed.

B. What if he says, "Don't tell my parents that I've been traveling with my girlfriend." Can/should you comply? This aspect demonstrates some of the complexities in this area of dealing with minors. The considerations applicable to advising parents of the minor child's whereabouts and safety do not necessarily apply to all the details, which in any event the consular officer may not have independent confirmation of. Certainly, there is no obligation to convey to 3rd parties, even parents, all known or suspected facts.

Scenario 5. The host government is on the phone. They have picked up a person bearing a U.S. passport and they suspect photo substitution in the passport. They are asking you to provide information about whether the passport number can be verified and whether it was reported lost or stolen. You check PIERS and CLASP and those automated records confirm the issuance of the passport and the fact that the person to whom it was issued reported it stolen.

A. Should you confirm that the passport was issued and reported stolen?
No. You may confirm that the passport was issued and reported stolen after you receive a written (faxed) request from the host government citing the reason for the request.

B. Should you request a written (faxed) request from the host government and then confirm that the passport was issued and reported stolen? Yes. You may confirm that the passport was issued and reported stolen after you receive a written (faxed) request from the host government citing the reason for the request.

C. Should you request a written (faxed) request from the host government and then direct the inquiry to the Department? You should not release any written record from PIERS or CLASP without authorization from CA/PPT/IML/R/RR. You may not testify or provide written statements for use in foreign proceedings without specific authorization from the Department.

Chapter IV

Foreign Affairs Manual
(FAM)

The following pages include excerpts from the Foreign Affairs Manual. As someone interested in the Foreign Service, you may find these pages interesting. Also, it may help you understand how to think about and respond to hypothetical situations. You can obtain the full FAM at www.state.gov.

The following are quoted paragraphs from the Consular Affairs section of the Foreign Affairs Manual (FAM). Reading these passages will provide you with an understanding of certain Embassy policies that will help you answer the hypothetical scenarios of the structured Interview. In addition, we believe that having a basic knowledge of the FAM is valuable in helping you learn more about the Foreign Service and the type of work you would be performing abroad. This is recommended reading for all candidates interested in joining the Foreign Service.

You can access the complete FAM at:
http://www.state.gov/m/a/dir/regs/fam/index.htm

A few important departments within the Department of State in Washington:

Bureau of Consular Affairs: Primary responsibility for protection of U.S. citizens abroad is carried out by the Bureau of Consular Affairs (CA) in the Department of State and by dedicated consular officers, locally engaged staff and consular agents abroad.

Overseas Citizens Services: Within CA, the Directorate of Overseas Citizens Services (CA/OCS) is charged with exercising the Secretary of State's responsibility to provide consular protection and services to United States citizens abroad. OCS serves as a liaison between concerned family members, friends and members of Congress in the U.S. and consular posts and U.S. citizens abroad.

CA/OCS is comprised of three offices: American Citizen Services and Crisis Management (ACS), Children's Issues (CI), and *Legal Affairs (L)*. These offices are under the leadership of a Managing Director and the Deputy Assistant Secretary for Overseas Citizens Services.

The Office of American Citizens Services (ACS) and Crisis Management (CA/OCS/ACS) is in effect the Department's "America Desk.'' ACS helps U.S. citizens abroad and their families and friends at home with emergencies such as deaths, arrests, illnesses and injuries. ACS provides vital assistance to U.S. citizens during periods of crisis such as transportation accidents, natural disasters, and civil unrest, including the evacuation of U.S. citizens.

The Office of Children's Issues (CA/OCS/CI) provides assistance to the public on international parental child abduction and international adoption cases.

The Office of Legal Affairs (*CA/OCS/L*) participates in formulating policies relating to emergency and non-emergency services to U.S. citizens residing or traveling abroad and to interested parties in the United States.

Consular Protection of U.S. Nationals Abroad

Eligibility

U.S. Nationals: Eligible for Consular Protection and Other Services

Lawful permanent resident aliens: LPRs have been lawfully accorded the privilege of residing permanently in the United States as immigrants in accordance with the immigration laws. LPRs generally are not entitled to emergency and protective services provided by the U.S. Government. Refer such persons to the nearest diplomatic representative of the country of which they are a national or citizen. When an LPR applicant has exceptionally close and strong ties to the United States, and overriding humanitarian and compassionate grounds exist, request guidance from CA/OCS/ACS about the propriety of providing the service, with the understanding that the host government may not, and is not obligated to, honor a request from the U.S. Government on behalf of such an individual.

No Ties to the United States: Persons with no ties or allegiance to the United States may not be provided emergency or protective services except under the most extraordinary circumstances, and then only with the prior approval of the Department

Welfare and Whereabouts of U.S. Nationals Abroad

This chapter outlines the Department policies, guidance, and procedures for locating U.S. citizens or nationals, determining their general welfare and/or assisting them when they encounter difficulties. Our most important function as consular officers is to protect and assist U.S. citizens or nationals traveling or residing abroad. The Department of State and the U.S. Congress place a high priority on our performing these protective services with sensitivity, tact, and the utmost proficiency.

Consular assistance to U.S. citizens or nationals in welfare and whereabouts matters includes, but is not limited to:

(1) Locating persons abroad who have lost touch with concerned parties in the United States;

(2) Locating persons abroad who are overdue for scheduled travel;

(3) Locating missing persons;

(4) Coordinating with host country and U.S. officials in search and rescue cases;

(5) Passing emergency family messages;

(6) Reporting on the general welfare of U.S. citizens or nationals, subject to the Privacy Act; and

(7) Providing emergency temporary refuge in limited cases.

Scope: During the course of other consular ACS work, such as arrest visits, emergency medical cases and child abuse cases, you will also use your welfare and whereabouts skills.

Limitations on you in handling welfare and whereabouts cases are as follows:
(1) You cannot compel a U.S. citizen/national to return to the United States, except when assisting law enforcement authorities to extradite a U.S. citizen/national fugitive;

(2) You cannot force a U.S. citizen/national to speak to or meet with you; and

(3) You cannot require a U.S. citizen/national to provide a reason for refusing to sign a Privacy Act waiver.

Overdue Arrival
Most U.S. citizens or nationals who have not traveled extensively do not realize that postal and telephone systems outside the United States do not always function well. When they do not hear from a close friend or relative who was due to arrive at a particular date and time, they may panic and seek help from the Department or a Foreign Service post. The person often calls home before the U.S. embassy or consulate can initiate a welfare and whereabouts search. CA/OCS/ACS asks inquiring family members to let us know when they hear from their relative so we may cancel the search. Sometimes, however, the person is not simply delayed or has not suddenly changed plans, but is really missing or in trouble. For this reason, consular officers must treat each request as a serious concern.

Sometimes information available to the consular officer is sketchy. The burden will fall on the consular officer to use imagination and contacts to locate the missing U.S. citizen or national. The search will be easier if you obtain as much information as possible from the caller. Consular officers may contact the Department to request additional information from passport or other records.

The Department will initiate welfare and whereabouts searches in response to inquiries from any family member. We do not require that the inquiry come from the next-of-kin, but recommend that families appoint a single point of contact. Requests initiated by bill collectors, private investigative firms, and casual acquaintances are not accepted. You should advise neighbors or people who may contact you after reading about the case that you are in contact with the family and providing all possible assistance, but that you cannot discuss the case due to Privacy Act considerations.

A consular check concerning the welfare and whereabouts of a U.S. citizen or national abroad usually focuses on the "whereabouts" issue. When the family knows where the person is located, but has concerns for the individual's welfare, there are a variety of options available to the consular officer to accomplish this task. Consular officers are not professional social workers, even if individual officers have background in that field. We cannot compel a person to permit a consular officer to observe a citizen or national, inspect the household, etc. Nevertheless, there are cases where it is imperative that the consular officer act quickly. This frequently requires close coordination with the host government. CA/OCS is available to assist you 24/7 in critical cases.

One may:
(1) Telephone the citizen/national who is the subject of the inquiry;

(2) Arrange for a visit to the person's home;

(3) Invite the person to come to the embassy or consulate to discuss his or her situation;

(4) Visit the individual personally; and

(5) Arrange for local authorities to visit the person.

If the person is located far away from the embassy or consulate, it may not be possible for you to visit the individual personally for some time. You may wish to:
(1) Arrange for local authorities to visit the person;

(2) Arrange for a visit by a member of the local American community, such as a warden; and

(3) Arrange for a visit from a nearby representative of consulate of a friendly nation.

Exercise "active listening" skills in conversations with the citizen/national. Consult CA/OCS/ACS for assistance or guidance.

The consular report of the visit should include a factual account of what occurred. Consider the following points in writing your report:

(1) Who visited the citizen;

(2) What were the conditions of the interaction – phone, in person, through a third party;

(3) When did it occur;

(4) Where did it occur;

(5) What did you observe;

(6) What was the person's demeanor;

(7) What did the person say about his or her situation;

(8) What are your concerns (if any) for the citizen/national's welfare; and

(9) What are your recommendations or questions?

Smart traveler enrollment of U.S. citizens

U.S. citizens may enroll in our Smart Traveler Enrollment Program (STEP). Enrollment is highly recommended; it is voluntary, however, not mandatory.

We encourage enrollment so that we may contact U.S. citizens in an evacuation or other emergency, to support the Department's efforts to protect U.S. nationals abroad.

Release of information obtained in this collection is subject to and restricted by the provisions of the Privacy Act (5 U.S.C. 552a).

Consular information program, messages for U.S. citizens, and the no double standard policy

The program consists of:
(1) Country Specific Information;

(2) Travel Alerts;

(3) Travel Warnings;

(4) Worldwide Cautions;

(5) Messages for U.S. Citizens, Security Messages for U.S. Citizens, and Emergency Messages for U.S, Citizens (hereafter all will be referred to as "Messages" unless there is a distinction to be made); and

(6) Fact Sheets

Dealing with your host government
Host country officials occasionally express dismay or resentment about the U.S. Government's public dissemination of security-related warnings. The Department has no higher responsibility than the safety and security of U.S. citizens. You may explain that U.S. law requires that we share information with U.S. citizens that will assist them to make prudent decisions about their own safety.

In certain situations, but **only with PRIOR PERMISSION from the Managing Director of CA/Overseas Citizens Services**, you may inform the host government of the imminent release of a Travel Warning. CA/OCS will coordinate Department permission in these cases. **Country Specific Information, Messages, Travel Alerts, and Travel Warnings are never subject to negotiation with or censoring by a foreign government.**

Statement of Policy

In administering the travel information program, the Department of State applies a "no double standard" policy to important security threat information, including criminal information.

(1)   Generally, if the Department shares information with the official U.S. community, it should also make the same or similar information available to the non-official U.S. community if the underlying threat applies to both official and non-official U.S. citizens/nationals.

(2)   If a post issues information to its employees about potentially dangerous situations, it should evaluate whether the potential danger could also affect private U.S. citizens/nationals living in or traveling through the affected area.

(3)   If so, the post should notify the Department and request approval of dissemination of the information to the public.

(4)   The policy is not intended to prevent the limited distribution of information about threats to specific U.S. citizens/ nationals or U.S. corporations. The Post may share important security information on a limited basis when directed toward a specific target or when appropriate to counter a particular threat.

Security Threats

The security threat information contained in Travel Alerts, Travel Warnings, Worldwide Cautions, and Messages is derived from threat information gathered from multiple sources, including our posts, the U.S. intelligence community, open sources, and our allies.

When security threat information is received, the relevant bureaus in the Department and other U.S. Government agencies attempt to evaluate whether a security threat is credible, specific (aimed at a particular individual or group and/or identifying a time and place), and non-counterable (cannot be avoided by taking appropriate measures).

If a threat evaluated as credible, specific, and non-counterable is targeted to a specific group or individual, and is unlikely to impact others, then the

Department, either directly or through post, may notify only that group or individual of the threat. For example, if easily identifiable members of the local U.S. community, such as employees of a particular company, are targeted, there would normally be no need to disseminate the threat information beyond the targeted group.

If a threat evaluated as credible, specific, and non-counterable is aimed at a broad group (e.g., U.S. citizens/nationals and/or U.S. interests generally), the Department will authorize the relevant post(s) to issue a Message, and may also issue or update a Travel Alert, Travel Warning, or Worldwide Caution.

Post's role

To ensure that the Department and posts avoid providing contradictory information on security threats to U.S. citizens/nationals, it is essential that post coordinate with the Department on dissemination of any information about potential threats to the safety and travel of U.S. citizens/nationals.

If you learn of a security threat, report it to the Department following the established procedures at your post. At this stage, you should not disseminate information about the threat beyond those with a "need to know" (i.e., persons who could develop additional information, help to counter the threat, or help assess appropriate dissemination) to avoid violating the "no double standard" policy. In the event the information is mistakenly disseminated to U.S. Government employees and/or others without a need to know, post should notify the Department immediately, with the post's senior consular officer responsible for ensuring that CA/OCS/ACS is among those notified.

If post believes that it should warn post personnel and/or issue a Security or Emergency Message, see 7 FAM 058 for what constitutes an Emergency Message for U.S. Citizens or Security Message for U.S. Citizens. When warning the local U.S. citizen/national community about a security threat, you should cable or email the basis for your concern, along with the proposed text of the message, to the Department via post's CA/OCS/ACS country officer.

If the Emergency or Security Message pertains to a threat so immediate that it cannot wait until Washington opening-of-business, clear your message with the CA/OCS duty officer, providing the proposed Message text.

Post may disseminate information about a threat without prior Department approval **ONLY** if immediate notice is critical to the security of U.S. citizens/nationals **and** there is no time to seek the Department's approval. These situations are exceedingly rare.

Remember that if post concludes it should warn its personnel or any U.S. Government employees, whether permanently stationed or on temporary duty abroad, about a security threat, the request for Department approval to warn post personnel should also include a request to share that same information with the non-official U.S. community under the "no double standard" policy.

The policy applies whether the information is shared with U.S. Government employees in town meetings, in post newsletters, by email, on the telephone, or by any other means.

Messages, security messages, and emergency messages for U.S. citizens
Along with Country Specific Information, Travel Alerts, and Travel Warnings, Messages for U.S. Citizens, Security Messages for U.S. Citizens, and Emergency Messages for U.S. Citizens (hereafter referred to as Messages unless there is a distinction to be made) are an important component of the Department's Consular Information Program.

There are three kinds of official local communications with our registered U.S. citizens:

(1)   You must use a "Message for U.S. Citizens" to disseminate information about routine topics such as voter registration, income tax season, new passport procedures, and other administrative/non-security issues of interest to the local U.S. citizen community.

(2)   You should use a "Security Message for U.S. Citizens" to communicate information about personal security threats of a general or systemic nature, or events/threats where local law-enforcement has taken measures to address or provide enhanced security to the general public. Such threats may include crime trends, demonstrations, peaceful actions intended to disrupt normal activity (i.e., strikes, sit-ins, marches), or localized events not likely to affect large numbers of U.S. citizens.

(3)   You should use an "Emergency Message for U.S. Citizens" to inform U.S. citizens about imminent events or threats that can affect their personal security and that may require immediate action by U.S. citizens on their own behalf, or by others, to ensure their safety. Emergency Messages may also be appropriate for threats to large numbers of U.S. citizens, circumstances where new developments to an existing security threat heighten the risks to U.S. citizens, or situations that put the life or safety of U.S. citizens in peril. This includes potentially violent demonstrations, civil disturbances, natural disasters, terrorist attacks, extraordinary measures by local authorities such as martial law, and other non-publicized breaking events. When the Department revises the Worldwide Caution, or issues a Travel Alert or Travel Warning for your country or region, you should disseminate it with an Emergency Message unless otherwise directed.

Posts have discretion in determining whether circumstances call for a Security Message or Emergency Message. However, to help promote consistency, CA/OCS makes the final determination when there are differences of opinion between posts and other offices outside the Bureau of Consular Affairs as to which type of message is most appropriate.

The Privacy Act and Americans Citizens Services

This section summarizes Privacy Act considerations applicable in consular protection cases and provides you general guidance and examples as to when you may release information that is otherwise protected. The Privacy Act is complicated, and not all aspects are discussed here. If you have any doubt about whether a disclosure of information about a U.S. citizen or lawful permanent resident (LPR) is permitted, you should contact CA/OCS/ACS. You do not have to contact CA/OCS for guidance in an emergency involving the health and safety of a U.S. citizen if there isn't time, or if you are merely confirming the U.S. citizenship of an individual for a U.S. or foreign law enforcement agency

The Privacy Act of 1974,

(1) Permits any U.S. citizen or lawful permanent resident (LPR) to access records about him or her contained in a Department of State "system of records," to learn about certain disclosures of those records, and to request amendment of any inaccuracies

(2) Requires the Department of State to identify each of its "systems of records" in the Federal Register. Virtually all American Citizens Services records are created and maintained in name retrievable systems of records, and have therefore been identified by the Department as "systems of records" subject to the Privacy Act.

(3) Prohibits the disclosure of records from a Privacy Act "system of records" by any method (written, oral, or electronic) unless the individual to whom the records pertain has consented, in writing to the disclosure.

(4) Requires that the Department keep a written accounting of many disclosures

(5) Prescribes civil remedies and criminal penalties for non-compliance.

U.S. citizens arrested/convicted overseas

Unless arrest and/or conviction records in post's host country are matters of public knowledge or have received widespread media attention locally or stateside, **you are not permitted under the Privacy Act to release information about an arrested and/or convicted U.S. citizen without either the latter's written permission** or a determination that the release of the information falls under one of the exceptions to the Privacy Act. When releasing information regarding an arrested U.S. citizen on the basis of the fact that his/her arrest and/or conviction are in the public domain, you should be very circumspect in what you disseminate to inquirers. Absent a Privacy Act waiver or Privacy Act exception, you should limit your responses to what is clearly in the public record - e.g., date and place of arrest and/or conviction and nature of the charges.

Information concerning the U.S. citizen's condition (physical, mental, or emotional), attorney, the U.S. citizen's correspondence with post, post's communications with host country government on behalf of the U.S. citizen, etc. **are not releasable** because such information relates to matters not generally viewed as being in the public domain. Posts have to be careful because at times, the media reports and repeats unconfirmed information, see 7 FAM 423.6 Arrests.

Deceased Individuals: The Privacy Act does not protect records pertaining to deceased individuals. However, next-of-kin may have a "common law" privacy interest in not having information about the deceased released, e.g., if it could embarrass, endanger or cause emotional distress to them.

Minors: The Privacy Act's protections apply to records pertaining to all U.S. citizens and LPRs, including minors. Information about a minor generally may be released to the minor's parent(s).

Parents, however, **do not have an absolute right to the information** under the Privacy Act and the wishes of the minor may, in some cases, override those of the parent(s). Normally, if you have been advised by a minor age 14 or older that he or she does not want any information released to a parent or guardian, you should honor those wishes absent the presence of compelling circumstances affecting the health or safety of the minor child. Bring the matter to the attention of CA/OCS immediately and we will provide an advisory opinion on a case-by-case basis.

Passport Records: You may confirm or deny the U.S. citizenship of an individual in response to a written request from a federal, state, local or foreign law enforcement agency where there is reason to believe the individual has violated the law. **You may not, however, release copies of passport records.** Refer requests for the release of copies of Passport Records to CA/PPT/ILM/R/RR, which has the responsibility for releasing such records.

Loss of Nationality: You may confirm a finding of loss of nationality to a foreign government. **You may not, however, release copies of Certificates of Loss of Nationality or related documents without consulting *CA/OCS/L* (*Ask-OCS-L-Dom-Post@state.gov*).** These questions frequently arise when a former U.S. citizen is seeking a high level position or elected political office in the host country.

Visa Records: The release of visa records with respect to U.S. citizens and LPRs is governed by the Privacy Act.

Relationship to the Freedom of Information Act (FOIA): While the Privacy Act allows U.S. citizens and LPRs to request access to name-retrievable records about themselves, the FOIA (5 U.S.C. 552) allows any "person" (including foreign citizens and governments, and business entities) to request access to any federal agency record. For purposes of consular work, two FOIA exceptions are most important. **First, the government is not required to disclose information to an individual that would amount to an unwarranted invasion of the privacy of a third party (i.e., the person who is not requesting the information).** For example, while records pertaining to deceased individual do not have any Privacy Act protections as noted above, a FOIA request for the decedent's file may be rejected in whole or in part where the release of information would unjustifiably invade the privacy of the latter's next-of-kin. **Second, records need not be released if their release is prohibited by another statute.** Thus, visa records are not releasable pursuant to the FOIA because of section 222(f) of the INA. The FOIA also includes exceptions for classified and pre-decisional or deliberative process documents, among others.

Privacy Act Waivers

Unless an exception applies, the Privacy Act requires "prior written consent of, the individual to whom the record pertains", before any such records can be released.

Form DS-5505, Authorization for Release of Information Under the Privacy Act, known colloquially as the Privacy Act Waiver, is the document to be used when seeking to obtain permission to release information on behalf of our citizens.

Obtaining a Privacy Act Waiver: You should not pressure (or appear to pressure) a U.S. citizen/non-citizen national to sign a Privacy Act Waiver (PAW). Explain the individual's Privacy Act rights. Also note that it may be helpful to advise that a waiver can help facilitate the Department's communication with family members and others potentially able to help, and that it is possible to limit the scope of the PAW so that it covers only certain people or categories of people. Then let the individual decide whether or not to sign the PAW.

Oral Waivers Not Acceptable: A faxed written waiver, which is followed by the signed original, can be accepted. An "oral" waiver, however, may not. Note that the absence of a written waiver does not preclude you from simply passing messages on behalf of a U.S. citizen. Thus, you can act upon a telephonic request from a U.S. citizen prisoner, for example, to relay a message to his attorney; however, a written waiver is required to transmit the prisoner's Privacy Act-protected file to that same attorney.

Waiver Duration And Applicability: The Privacy Act is silent as to the temporal duration and scope of a Privacy Act waiver; however, as a general rule, the Department considers that a waiver granted in connection with a specific incident - e.g., arrest or illness – is limited to the duration of the incident. Thus, for example, an individual who waives his/her Privacy Act rights in the context of an illness is not deemed to have waived his/her rights with respect to a subsequent and unrelated illness.

There are several circumstances in which information from any of the Department's systems of records may be released to law enforcement agencies:

- Information regarding "a violation or potential violation of law, whether civil, criminal, or regulatory in nature," may be "referred to the appropriate agency, whether federal, state, local or foreign," responsible for the alleged violation

- Information may be disclosed "to a Federal, State, local or foreign agency" in response to such an agency's written request "where there is reason to believe that an individual has violated the law," but "only to the extent necessary to enable such agency to discharge its responsibilities" with respect to the alleged violation

- Information may be disclosed to a federal agency (but not a state, local, or foreign agency) "for the integration and use of such information to protect against terrorism, if that record is about one or more individuals known, or suspected, to be or to have been involved in activities constituting, in preparation for, in aid of, or related to terrorism".

This **does not mean** that other government agencies have unfettered access to consular files. **Under these routine uses:**

You may routinely give the Internal Revenue Service (IRS) information concerning the current address of a taxpayer who is the subject of either a tax investigation or action to collect taxes owed

You may verify U.S. citizenship/nationality or a finding of loss of U.S. nationality to a host government immigration or social security authority in response to a written request. You **may not** release a copy of a passport or Report of Birth application from PIERS or other records.

Health or safety exception

The Privacy Act's "health or safety" exception allows disclosure of information without a PAW "**to a person pursuant to a showing of compelling circumstances affecting the health or safety of an individual if upon such disclosure notification is transmitted to the last known address of such individual**".

Only Emergencies – Don't Use Health and Safety as a Catchall: You should not use this exception as a catchall to release information when it seems the "expedient" or the "right" thing to do. In most instances, an individual's privacy must be safeguarded.

Circumstances Affecting Health or Safety: This exception requires **"showing compelling circumstances affecting the health or safety of an individual".** This section of the Act may be invoked to save the life of the U.S. citizen/national, notwithstanding his/her written affirmation of his/her right to privacy. You are also permitted to disclose Privacy Act-protected information about an individual in order to remove that person from harm's way. In determining whether the "health or safety" exception is applicable in any given case, you should consider what reasonable course of action would safeguard the welfare of an individual whose physical or mental well-being is at stake in light of all the relevant circumstances - i.e., age of individual, nature of condition, availability of medical facilities, degree to which individual and/or local health facilities can communicate with next-of-kin or friends stateside, etc.

Persons To Whom Information May Be Released: Information may be released to any person who can reasonably be expected to assist the individual whose health or safety is at risk, e.g., relative, friend, attorney, clergyman, member of Congress, etc.

Notification: When information is disclosed pursuant to the "health or safety" exception, the individual who is the subject of the released information must be notified of the disclosure in writing. Therefore, whenever you make a "health or safety" disclosure, you should advise *CA/OCS/L* and provide any information about the individual's last known address so that *CA/OCS/L* may attempt to effect the requisite notification.

"Health or Safety" of a Third Party: The individual about whom records are disclosed need not be the individual whose health or safety is at peril. Thus, for example, a Privacy Act-protected record about an individual can be released to a physician treating a third person if it can be shown that the latter's illness is in some way linked to the individual who is the subject of the Privacy Act-protected record.

Incompetency Determination: In a true health or safety emergency, the health or safety exception can be invoked **regardless of whether a person has been declared incompetent, or is experiencing mental problems**, etc. A judicial determination of incompetency is **not required** to release information. The relevant standard is that the mental problems preclude the person from making rational decisions about his/her self-interest.

Missing Persons

A missing person is a citizen or national who has not arrived at a location on the scheduled date and time.

Examples of Missing Persons Cases:
- U.S. citizen known to have started to climb a mountain, but who never returned
- U.S. citizen skier who disappeared after a run down a dangerous slope marked "dangerous" by the ski patrol
- U.S. citizen on a day excursion boat trip who never returned
- Developmentally challenged U.S. citizen adult who slipped away from care giver and disappeared
- U.S. citizen participating in protest in host country who disappeared and may be held by local authorities or rival groups.

Preliminary inquiries

You should initiate a welfare and whereabouts check. For example:
(1)   Check the consular section's registration, Internet Based Registration System (IBRS), ACS systems for addresses or telephone numbers;

(2)   Check with local contacts or local addresses that the inquirer has provided;

(3)   Contact the local immigration authorities to determine if they have any record of entry or departure for the person in question;

(4)   Contact the local police department (foreigners division) to ask if it has any information on the missing person and to alert it to the problem;

(5)   Contact the National Tourist Bureau;

(6)   Check with appropriate hotels;

(7)   Check with airlines;

(8)   Check with local U.S. community leaders and associations; and

(9)   Contact local hospitals.

Broadening search

If these checks fail to produce any information on the missing person and the Department has been informed of this and requests further efforts be made:

(1)   File a formal missing person's report with police;

(2)   Check with the coroner's office for unidentified bodies;

(3)   Ask for local media coverage gratis;

(4)   Contact wardens, missionary groups, etc.;

(5)   Ask the Peace Corps Director to alert volunteers;

(6)   Follow up any requests to local agencies to ensure that they conduct a thorough investigation; and

(7)   Contact consular officers of other countries who may have other contacts in remote locations.

Working with families, employers, and friends

If the U.S. citizen/national's last known location was in a foreign country, it is not unusual for family, employers, and friends to travel to the scene. Posts should assist these individuals as much as possible. The CA/OCS Intranet site includes a variety of information that you may wish to refer to including guidance for families dealing with the media and working with local authorities. **Keep in mind:**

(1)   If the host country establishes a hotline or point of contact for families, let the Department know so we may relay this information to families in the United States;

(2)   CA/OCS/ACS may have an ad hoc team working on the incident, responding to family inquiries. It is useful to know what is going

> on at the scene and how you have been helping families and victims;

(3)   Try to establish a caseworker approach in which one consular officer at the post is the primary point of contact with one designated family member; and

(4)   Keep good records of your conversations.

Cooperation with private investigators retained by family

Families may retain the services of private investigators, companies using search dogs, and other services to attempt to locate the missing person. Posts should cooperate with such persons as much as possible and assist them in contacting local authorities. If post maintains a list of local private search and rescue organizations, it should be provided to the family.

Family abuse situations

It is not unusual for posts to encounter situations involving allegations of abusive family relationships. This may include troubled marriages, domestic violence, child abuse and even elder abuse. The traditional consular role of conducting welfare and whereabouts checks is more complicated in these cases. You are not simply being asked to locate a citizen/national and confirm that he or she is all right and ask the person to contact his or her family in the United States. When a post or the Department receives an allegation of family abuse and we are asked to conduct a welfare and whereabouts check, we must consider whether a visit by the consular officer could put the person in greater danger, and whether it would be appropriate to seek assistance from the host government. Consular officers are not professional social workers, even if individual officers have background in that field. We cannot compel a family to permit a consular officer to observe a citizen or national or inspect the household, school, etc. The family's cooperation with consular officers is purely voluntary. Nevertheless, there are cases where it is imperative that the consular officer act quickly. This frequently requires close coordination with the host government.

Arrest of U.S. Citizens Abroad

One of the most important functions of consular officers is to protect and assist private U.S. citizens or nationals traveling or residing abroad. Few of our citizens need that assistance more than those who have been arrested in a foreign country or imprisoned in a foreign jail.

(1)   Neither arrest nor conviction deprives a U.S. citizen of the right to the consular officer's best efforts in protecting the citizen's legal rights. As consular officers we must assist arrested or imprisoned

U.S. citizens with dedicated professionalism, regardless of any private views as to their guilt or the heinousness of the crime.

(2)   You must also remember that there are potential flaws in any judicial system, and must remain alert for them. If you have valid reason to believe that an U.S. citizen or national has been arrested or charged unjustly, for political, monetary, or other reasons, you should continue to handle the case as an arrest case. You should also bring your opinion and information to the attention of the Department and post senior management immediately, since this adds a dimension to the case that may demand unusual action in the political or judicial arena.

(3)   Although you are the primary action officer in arrest cases, you may need help from other post officers in making prison visits, in attending trials, and in cultivating rapport with, and gaining the cooperation of, local law enforcement officials. This is especially true at posts where consular resources are limited and the consular workload is heavy. You should not hesitate in making your needs known to post management, and encourage such cooperation whenever possible.

Prepare prisoner visitation kits

If your post's arrest volume warrants, put together one or more attaché case(s) containing everything required for a visit. This is particularly useful when officers from other than ACS or the Consular Section make visits.

Items may include:
(1)   List of important contact numbers (Prison wardens, Police supervisors, etc.);

(2)   Prisoner Interview Checklist;

(3)   Lawyers' List;

(4)   Judicial Procedure Information;

(5)   Privacy Act Waiver forms

(6)   Affidavit forms (used in the event of mistreatment or similar circumstances);

(7)   Passport applications;

(8)   EMDA Loan forms;

(9)   Camera (If permitted); and

(10)   Personal items for Prisoner: If local circumstances warrant, and if allowed, consider putting some necessities in a clear plastic bag to give to prisoner on your first visit. This could include: soap, toothbrush and toothpaste, comb, deodorant/antiperspirant,

hygiene products, writing paper, pen or pencil, magazines or other reading material, dry food, such as an energy bar, granola bar, etc.

Notification

In order for you to perform your consular protective functions in an efficient and timely manner, it is essential that you receive prompt notification from local authorities whenever a U.S. citizen or national is arrested, although, as explained below, local authorities are not always required to inform you. Prompt notification is the necessary first step in obtaining early access to the arrestee and therefore you should take all steps to make sure you have good relationships with host country law enforcement contacts.

Although the legal responsibility to give consular notification may rest with the arresting authorities, as a practical matter, you should take steps to create a working atmosphere conducive to prompt notifications. Actions on your part could include developing local relationships.

Access

Consular officers must make every effort to gain prompt personal access to an arrested U.S. citizen or national for a number of reasons:

(1)   Experience demonstrates that requesting prompt, personal access to the U.S. citizen or national assures both the arrestee and the host authorities of the serious interest of the U.S. Government in the case.

(2)   Anything less than your full efforts to obtain prompt access undermines our insistence that host country arresting authorities notify a U.S. consular officer without delay following the arrest.

(3)   Experience shows that abuse of a prisoner is most likely during the early arrest and pre-trial detention stages. Your prompt access to the detainee can often forestall physical abuse of the prisoner by the arresting and/or investigating authorities.

(4)   In instances where abuse has, or is alleged to have, already occurred, your prompt access to the prisoner permits possible visible verification and puts you in the best position to demand medical attention and/or verification, as well as demand a prompt investigation by appropriate authorities.

(5)   You can provide the arrestee with a list of reputable lawyers or information concerning local legal aid before the arrestee selects a lawyer who may not have the requisite level of competence.

(6)   You have the opportunity to explain the legal and judicial procedures of the host government and the detainee's rights under that government at a time when such information is most useful.

First contact

Upon receiving notification that a U.S. citizen or national is being detained, it is absolutely essential that you achieve timely access to the detainee through one of the following methods:

Personal Visit: As consular officer, you are required to visit the arrestee as soon as possible following receipt of consular notification or information about the arrest from another source, such as the arrestee's family or the media.

Telephone Contact: If a personal visit by an officer within 24 hours is not possible, you should contact the detainee by telephone. You should ask the detaining authorities to permit a private conversation. (In some countries the authorities are required to allow private conversations; see Consular Notification and Access Manual, p. 34, for the list.) Such contact does not eliminate your responsibility to follow up with a personal visit at the earliest possible opportunity, normally within a few days.

Visit By A Consular Agent: If a consular officer cannot do so, a Consular Agent should visit the arrestee promptly. Posts that have consular agents assigned within their districts should make maximum use of them in protecting the legal and human rights of incarcerated U.S. citizens and assuring their welfare. As a guide to what consular agents may be expected to do in such instances, posts should consult the Consular Agents' Handbook.

Visit by Volunteers: If an immediate personal visit by an officer or Consular Agent is not possible, you may consider enlisting cooperation of U.S. citizens residing in the area of the place of arrest to visit the detained U.S. citizen or national.

Verification of Citizenship and Identity

Before rendering any substantial service to an arrestee, you must determine that the individual is a U.S. citizen national or otherwise entitled to the protection of the U.S. Government.

Detecting Apparent or Alleged Abuse

This is often your best opportunity to question the prisoner about his/her treatment by authorities, examine him/her closely for signs of abuse, and take any statement he/she wish to make on the matter.

Explaining Your Role

Give the arrestee a realistic and positive understanding of your interest in and responsibility for a U.S. citizen or national in this situation.

    (1)   It is useful at this point to make clear to the prisoner that the judicial system and personal rights he or she enjoyed in the United States do not apply abroad.

    (2)   Explain that a U.S. citizen or national is entitled to claim consular protection abroad, regardless of evidence of guilt, the nature of the alleged crime, or the status of the citizen.

    (3)   While it is only fair to curb the prisoner's expectations that consular assistance will result in extraordinary intervention or miraculous remedies, you can and should emphasize the actions that can be taken on the arrestee's behalf.

    (4)   Avoid any display of disdain, self-righteousness, or moral disapproval that might impair the relationship with the arrestee.

Delivering Attorneys List

Provide the arrestee with a current list of attorneys that might be available to him/her. Explain you cannot recommend an attorney, but that you can point out those on the list who speak English, and those who either have some past experience in, or who have indicated a willingness to, defend a U.S. citizen or national accused of the same or similar crimes. Alternatively, provide the arrestee with an abbreviated list of those who speak English, have past experience in or are willing to defend a U.S. citizen or national accused of same or similar crimes.

Outlining the Judicial System

Briefly explain to the prisoner the highlights of the judicial system within which the arrestee must work, and provide a written description that covers this topic in detail, including initial arrest, remand procedure, trial procedure, appeal process, and penal conditions and rules.

Obtaining Privacy Act Consent

Because U.S. citizens or nationals or LPRs arrested abroad usually have family or friends who will inquire about the arrestee, you should attempt to obtain a Privacy Act consent from the prisoner to pass information to persons likely to have an interest in the arrest. Such persons might include parents, brothers or sisters, close friends, attorneys, members of Congress, or the media. See Form DS-5505. It should be noted that this form is a guide to obtaining written consent, although other methods of clear written consent may also be acceptable.

Identifying Family and Persons to Contact

Advise the prisoner you will contact his or her next of kin, or other family or friends the arrestee designates. Often the arrestee may initially not wish to notify anyone, usually hoping for an early release. In this case, assure him/her that you will not contact anyone without his/her consent, but encourage him/her to provide the contact information anyway, so you have it available if he/she later changes his/her decision.

A heterosexual or same-sex partner of the arrestee who was in a civil union or similar arrangement recognized by a U.S. jurisdiction will be treated the same as a "spouse" for purposes of this FAM section.

Protecting Prisoner's Personal Property

In most countries, it is the practice of arresting officials to confiscate the personal property (such as money, clothing, watches, rings, computers, automobiles) of newly arrested persons. Often no receipts are given for these items, and, with no records, the items may disappear.

During the initial visit to a U.S. citizen or national arrestee, you should ask the prisoner if the arresting authorities took any personal property, including a passport, and, if so, whether a signed and dated receipt was given in exchange. If the arresting authority did not follow these procedures, you should take immediate steps to determine the whereabouts of the confiscated items and to obtain a receipt acknowledging custody from the local authorities. Prompt action is necessary if the items are to be located and retrieved.

You should not assume responsibility for holding or storing personal property or money on behalf of an arrestee

Providing Minimal Personal Comfort Items

If such items are not normally provided the prisoner by arresting authorities, you should provide: soap, toothbrush and toothpaste, comb, deodorant/antiperspirant, hygiene products, writing paper, pen or pencil, magazines or other reading material, dry food, such as an energy bar, granola bar, etc.

Photographing The Prisoner

Although not a requirement, the Department strongly recommends taking a few photos of the arrestee, as long as the host country authorities permit the taking of photos and the arrestee consents. These photos often prove useful for a number of reasons:

(1)   They may serve as evidence in validating and protesting any allegations of physical abuse.

(2)   They may help in identification and citizenship verification when there is reason to suspect the prisoner is using a false identity.

(3)   They can provide some reassurance to family members regarding the arrestee's health and welfare.

Generally one full-length and one passport-style close-up photograph is sufficient. If there are signs of abuse, or injuries sustained during the actual arrest, also photograph any bruises, cuts, abrasions etc. closely and carefully.

Obligation of Host Government to Allow Visit
Even when a foreign national arrestee has not requested a consular visit, the prison authorities must give consular officers access to the arrestee upon request and permit them to communicate with him/her, and to arrange for legal representation. If the arrestee does not want your assistance, you should insist to the prison authorities that they allow you the opportunity to confirm this fact directly through a face-to-face visit.

Reporting an Arrest
It is imperative that you submit prompt and comprehensive reports in the American Citizen Services (ACS) automated system on the arrest and detention of any U.S. citizen or national that involves any one of the following factors:

(1)   Detention over 24 hours;

(2)   Physical abuse or denial of human rights; or

(3)   Circumstances that in your judgment involve special public relations or human rights considerations.

Crime Victim Assistance

The Bureau of Consular Affairs created the Crime Victim Assistance Program (applies to U.S. Citizens/nationals only) because the needs of victims of serious or violent crimes overseas are notably different from cases involving accidents, illness, or death by natural causes due to the nature of the trauma the victim experiences and involvement in the criminal justice process.

Serious crimes include: homicide, sexual assault, child physical and sexual abuse, domestic violence, armed robbery, assault, kidnapping, other crimes in which the victim suffers serious physical injuries and/or emotional trauma.

Role Of The Consular Officer: Physical safety of the victim and his or her sense of security are your most important concerns.

In many serious crime cases abroad, the victims and/or family and friends look to you for assistance because they do not know how things work in a foreign country. You must be empathetic and understanding when helping either the victim or his/her family or friend. They are undoubtedly scared, frustrated and emotionally distraught trying to deal with their problems in an unfamiliar, foreign environment with none of their usual support systems available.

The Consular Section should prepare a handout, cleared by CA/OCS/ACS, explaining the criminal justice system in your country. Also include what you can do for the victim so he/she will have written information to review and help him/her make the necessary decisions. Post the handout on your Web site because some victims choose not to report the assault to you, but may still need assistance and information.

Quick Reference Checklist:

(1) Establish immediate contact with the victim or in the event the victim dies, the victim's family;

(2) Express empathy that the victimization occurred or condolences for the family's loss, and validate their reactions to the traumatic event;

(3) Report the incident to CA/OCS/ACS immediately by telephone followed by a cable;

(4) Establish a proactive "case-worker approach" in which the victim or family talks primarily to one person who is responsible for communication about the case. An officer in CA/OCS/ACS responsible for the region will facilitate communication with the post as necessary;

(5) Assess and address safety issues and immediate emergency medical and physical needs of the victim in coordination with local authorities;

(6) Assist the victim with immediate basic needs, such as shelter, food and clothing;

(7) Involve local crime victim assistance specialty programs where available and appropriate, e.g., rape crisis intervention, child protective services, shelters for battered women, and other victim support schemes;

(8) Consult with CA/OCS/ACS to identify additional services that can be provided, including referral to specialized victim assistance programs and crime victim compensation in the United States;

(9) Assist the victim with making a police report;

(10) Ascertain the status of the police investigation into the incident and request a copy of the police report to provide to the victim, with translation if possible;

(11) Assist the victim with the practical consequences of the crime, such as facilitating contact with family and/or arranging for a prompt return home;

(12) Help the victim regain control of his/her life by providing information about what to expect in the immediate future (anticipated treatment, changes in hotel arrangements, law enforcement action and how the return of recovered stolen property is handled, etc.);

(13) Provide the victim with written information about the host country's criminal justice process and points of contact for additional information about the host government.

You Can	You Cannot
• Listen to the citizen's report of what happened and provide information about help in accessing local sources of assistance	• Act as a social worker, counselor or legal adviser
• Observe the citizen's behavior, words, and demeanor and offer appropriate assistance.	• Pledge the expenditure of U.S. Government funds in payment of expenses for transport or care for a patient beyond what is available under the Repatriation/EMDA programs
• Report the case to CA/OCS/ACS in objective terms	
• Coordinate with host country authorities, making appropriate representations on behalf of the citizen	
• Provide the citizen with written information about resources for crime victims available in the United States	
• Relay information to family, friends, Congressional offices, etc., consistent with the Privacy Act. See the CA/OCS Intranet Privacy Act Feature	
• Provide financial assistance to citizens through OCS Trust monies sent by family or friends and Repatriation/EMDA loan programs	

Are there limitations on consular officers regarding victims of crimes and disclosure of information (privacy act)?

Information contained in a name-retrievable system of records concerning a U.S. citizen/national victim of a crime may not be disclosed by any means of communication to any person, or to another agency except:

(1) By written authorization by the individual who is the subject of the record; and

(2) In accordance with the 12 exceptions to the conditions of disclosure in the Privacy Act.

In a victim of crime situation, disclosure could be permissible under one of the following statutory exceptions:

(1) "for a routine use" published in the Federal Register; or

(2) "to a person pursuant to a showing of compelling circumstances affecting the health or safety of an individual if upon such disclosure notification is transmitted to the last known address of such individual."

The health and safety exception of the Privacy Act (5 U.S.C. 552a(b)(8) makes it possible to release information about the victim of a serious crime without a Privacy Act waiver. The information, however, can only be released to those who can reasonably be expected to assist the U.S. citizen victim and a notification of disclosure must be sent to the last known address of the victim.

Emergencies/Crisis FAQs *(as provided by the Department of State)*

Q: What is the Department of State's role during a crisis overseas? Do you always evacuate U.S. citizens during a crisis overseas?

A: The actions we take depend on the nature of the crisis. In some instances, we may only need to provide information on conditions in the country, such as warning about areas of unrest, how and where to seek help, and other useful advice. In more serious situations, we may recommend that U.S. citizens leave the foreign country, and, if commercial transportation is not available, provide departure assistance, as our resources permit.

Q: What departure assistance do you provide? Why do you tell U.S. citizens they should leave, and then don't offer transportation?

A: The assistance we provide depends upon the nature of the crisis. Regularly scheduled commercial flights or transportation are always the best option when local communications and transportation infrastructure are intact and operating normally, even if we have advised all U.S. citizens to leave. Our efforts are devoted to keeping the local U.S. citizen community informed of developments and travel options.

Q: What happens during an evacuation?

A: Each evacuation depends on the nature of the crisis. In extreme situations, where local infrastructure is damaged or severely compromised, we work with the host government, other countries, and other U.S. government agencies to arrange chartered or non-commercial transportation for U.S. citizens seeking to depart. This could include transportation by air, land, or sea. While we partner closely with the Department of Defense, military options are only used as a last resort. You should not expect the U.S. military to assist you when we issue a Travel Warning advising you to leave a country.

Q: Why don't you use the U.S. military in every evacuation?

A: We use the resources that are most expedient and appropriate to the situation. Expectations of rescue by helicopters, the U.S. military, and U.S. government-provided transportation with armed escorts reflect a Hollywood script more than reality. While some evacuations involve U.S. military or other U.S. government assets, most rely on commercial transportation and local infrastructure. Any level of departure assistance constitutes an enormous logistical effort.

Q: Will the U.S. government come and pick me up if I need assistance getting to the airport or other evacuation point?

A: Crises place an enormous strain on our resources as embassy personnel focus on assisting U.S. citizens affected by the crisis. Security conditions can also limit our ability to move freely around the country. It is almost impossible for the U.S. government to provide in-country transportation service to individuals or specific groups during a foreign crisis. You should therefore pay close heed to our travel and safety information for the country you are traveling to or residing in, monitor local conditions, and have a plan of action in case of emergency.

Q: Will the U.S. government pay for my travel? How much will it cost?

A: Departure assistance is expensive. U.S. law 22 U.S.C. 2671(b) (2) (A) requires that any departure assistance be provided "on a reimbursable basis to the maximum extent practicable." This means that evacuation costs are ultimately your responsibility; you will be asked to sign a form promising to repay the U.S. government. We charge you the equivalent of a full coach fare on commercial air at the time that commercial options cease to be a viable option. You will be taken to a nearby safe location, where the traveler will need to make his or her own onward travel arrangements. If you are destitute, and private resources are not available to cover the cost of onward travel, you may be eligible for emergency financial assistance.

Q: What about my pets? Will the U.S. government transport them?

A: In general, we are not able to provide transportation assistance for your pets. If the pet can fit into an under-the-seat carrier, it can accompany the traveler. U.S. citizens traveling or residing abroad with pets should make alternate plans for their care or commercial transport if a crisis occurs abroad.

Q: How can I receive updated information during a crisis?

A: We encourage all U.S. citizens traveling abroad, especially citizens who plan to be overseas for a significant amount of time, to enroll in the Smart Traveler Enrollment Program (STEP). It is important that you keep your contact information up-to-date so that we can notify you or your designated emergency contact of developments and provide valuable information.

Also be sure to monitor our website, www.travel.state.gov, for updates, as this is our primary tool to disseminate important information during a crisis. Our Facebook and Twitter accounts are also good sources of information. Rest assured that in case of a crisis, we will make use of all available modes of communication to keep our citizens informed, including the internet, social media, TV, and radio.

Q: If I don't hear from the embassy or I'm not enrolled in STEP, can I call them?

A: Often our embassies and consulates abroad cannot handle the huge volume of calls that follow a major crisis. We encourage you to contact us using the Task Force Alert (see below for more details), special e-mail addresses established for public inquiries during a crisis, or our U.S.-based telephone number at 1-888-407-4747 (from overseas +1-202-501-4444).

Q: What is Task Force Alert? How can I provide information about myself or my U.S. citizen friends and loved ones who are affected by a crisis overseas?

A: The best way to contact us during a major crisis overseas is via Task Force Alert, a free service that allows U.S. citizens to enter information about themselves or their U.S. citizens friends and loved ones into a database that we use to provide emergency consular assistance to U.S. citizens during a crisis. This service does not automatically alert emergency medical or law enforcement officials. U.S. citizens experiencing an emergency that requires immediate medical or law enforcement response should contact appropriate local responders. It is only applicable to U.S. citizens who are in the affected foreign country, and we do not collect information on people who are not U.S. citizens.

Q: What if I don't have access to e-mail or phone?

A: We know that Internet and cell phone service is sometimes interrupted during a crisis. Land line phones might also be affected. In such cases, we will use local television and radio to broadcast emergency information and may also use a system of pre-designated U.S. citizen "wardens" to pass on information to other U.S. citizens in your area. We also encourage citizens to reach out to family and friends outside the affected area to obtain information and relay messages to and from the task force handling the crisis at the Department of State. Don't underestimate the power of social media – regularly updating your status through social media sites is an effective way to let your loved ones know how you are doing.

Q: What about my family and friends who are not U.S. citizens? Will you help them depart the country?

A: During a crisis, our priority is assisting U.S. citizens. You should not expect to bring friends or relatives who are not U.S. citizens on U.S. government chartered or non-commercial transportation. Exceptions may be made to accommodate special family circumstances, such as when the spouse of a U.S. citizen is a legal permanent resident, or "green card" holder; however, it is the non-U.S. citizen's responsibility to be sure he or she has appropriate travel documentation for the destination location. Any services provided to non-U.S. citizens are on a space-available basis after U.S. citizens are accommodated.

Q: If my U.S. passport is expired, will you still assist me?

A: We strongly recommend that all U.S. citizens traveling or residing abroad keep their travel documents up-to-date. If your U.S. passport expires, you may be required to obtain a valid emergency travel document from the nearest U.S. embassy or consulate before traveling. In some cases, we may need to take additional steps to determine your citizenship.

> **Q:** What happens to visa processing during a crisis?

A: In a crisis, our priority is assisting U.S. citizens. Depending on the nature and extent of the crisis, visa processing could be limited or suspended.

Housing Abroad Policy

U.S. citizen employees assigned to U.S. missions abroad may be provided housing. Such housing may be provided in U.S. Government-owned or leased properties, or through the living quarters allowance (LQA) and military overseas housing allowance (OHA) programs. The objective of the housing program is to provide safe and secure housing that is adequate to meet the personal and professional requirements of employees at a cost most advantageous to the U.S. Government. For the purposes of this policy, adequate housing is defined as that comparable to what an employee would occupy in the Washington, DC Metropolitan Area, with adjustments for family size and locality abroad.

The chief of mission (COM), or the single real property manager (SRPM) as the COM's designee, is responsible for ensuring that the preventive, routine, and special maintenance programs are implemented and that all properties occupied by employees serving under the COM are free of hazardous conditions that could affect the health or safety of people. For USAID-owned or leased property, the USAID executive officer is responsible for establishing and implementing preventive, routine, and special maintenance programs.

Responsibilities of the State Department:
(1) Clean, service, repair, and restore plumbing systems, swimming pools, electrical and mechanical systems, heating and air conditioning systems, and major building systems (e.g., elevators);
(2) Maintain interiors and exteriors of buildings and structures, including painting, patching, replacing windows, caulking, etc.;
(3) Perform repairs required due to reasonable wear and tear;
(4) Perform repairs of damage to residential property except for occupant responsibilities (see below); and
(5) Clean and air vacant residential units and keep their exterior grounds in readiness for future occupancy.

Responsibility of the tenant/FSO:
Occupants of U.S. Government-held residences are responsible for maintaining them in presentable condition and returning them to the U.S. Government in clean and habitable condition. Posts must issue, as part of

the post housing guide, uniform rules detailing these responsibilities. The responsibilities should conform to what is normally expected of an occupant who leases residential quarters in the United States. Posts should prepare a written statement of employee responsibilities to be signed upon occupancy.

Occupants are responsible for activities such as light bulb replacement, routine daily user care of swimming pools (chemicals, water PH (percentage of Hydrogen), cleaning, filling, etc.), seasonal care of walks and driveways (e.g., snow removal), and periodic cleaning of window air conditioning filters, appliances (e.g., refrigerators, freezers, ranges).

Occupants are responsible for repairs required by deliberate acts or by the negligence of the occupant, family, guests, employees, or other members of the employee's household.

The U.S. Government will supply furniture, furnishings, appliances, and equipment (FFA&E) as determined by the post, from the approved lists of FFA&E in 15 FAM Exhibit 723A, for U.S. Government-held residences of U.S. citizen employees (direct-hire or personal services contractors) hired in the United States.

Standard items for U.S. government-furnished residences include:
- Furniture includes: Sofas, Chairs, Dining and kitchen tables, Desks, Buffets, Coffee and end tables, Bookcases, China cabinets, Mirrors, Beds (including mattresses, box springs and frames), Wardrobes (as needed), Bureaus, Side tables, Dressers, Rugs, carpets, and carpet pads, Table and floor lamps, and normal lighting fixtures, Draperies, curtains, blinds, or shades
- Appliances includes: Cooking range (gas or electric), Refrigerator, Washing machine and dryer, or shared laundry facilities, Smoke detectors, Fire extinguishers, initial set of electric light bulbs, Electrical regulators, such as transformers and adaptor plugs, as necessary for U.S. Government-furnished equipment

Chapter V

Practice Test I

Job Knowledge Test

We recommend that you take this test under the same constraints you will have in the exam. Take the whole test within 40 minutes, without bathroom breaks. You have an average of 40 seconds per question (60 questions). Do not use a calculator, as they will not be allowed in the exam. Remember that the Department of State does not deduct points for wrong answers; if you are unsure about an answer, make an educated guess.

The Job Knowledge Test will incorporate questions on the following topics: U.S. Government, U.S. History, U.S. Society and Culture, World History and Geography, Economics, Mathematics and Statistics, Management, Communications and Computers.

Our practice exams are more heavily weighted toward U.S. Government, U.S. History, and World History and Geography because we believe that these are the easiest topics for which you can study (i.e., many of the other topics include basic or general knowledge). These topics will likely encompass 40%-60% the questions in the actual exam, which will have a more questions on the other categories, particularly management topics.

Q1   Which of the following diplomats designed the policy of containment with the Soviet Union?

(A)   Richard Haass
(B)   Richard Holbrooke
(C)   George Kennan
(D)   Henry Kissinger

Q2   Which of the following countries is located in the area known as the Cradle of Civilization in the fertile crescent?

(A)   Iraq
(B)   Greece
(C)   Egypt
(D)   Italy

Q3   The current U.S. system of four time zones was established in 1883. Which of the following organizations created the time zone system?

(A)   Congress
(B)   The railroads
(C)   Wells Fargo
(D)   The telegraph companies

Q4   In 1951, this country was the first country to achieve independence through the United Nations, when it became a constitutional and hereditary monarchy. The country has the largest oil reserves in Africa. Which country is this?

(A)   Nigeria
(B)   Libya
(C)   Angola
(D)   Saudi Arabia

Q5　The Triangle Shirtwaist factory is best known for which of the following reasons:

(A)　It is the last remaining operating factory in New York's garment district

(B)　The first major outsourcing operation

(C)　A major strike in the early 20th century

(D)　A fire that killed 146 people in the early 20th century

Q6　The Shinto religion is a major religion in which of these countries?

(A)　Thailand

(B)　Japan

(C)　Malaysia

(D)　Myanmar

Q7　The Canadian company Research in Motion is best known for which of the following:

(A)　Smart phones

(B)　Electric Vehicles

(C)　Software

(D)　Renewable energy

Q8　Which of the following countries is a former Italian colony that has the largest crude oil reserves in Africa?

(A)　Mali

(B)　Gabon

(C)　Nigeria

(D)　Libya

Q9　Which of the following is the most populous Arab nation?

(A)　Saudi Arabia

(B)　Egypt

(C)　Indonesia

(D)　Iraq

Q10 The model of delivering computer services over the internet using shared servers and software is an example of which of the following:

(A) Grid computing
(B) Data warehouse computing
(C) Autonomic computing
(D) Cloud computing

Q11 Which of the following is the largest daily newspaper in the United States by circulation?

(A) USA Today
(B) Los Angeles Times
(C) Wall Street Journal
(D) New York Times

Q12 Which of the following countries has the largest Muslim population?

(A) Indonesia
(B) Saudi Arabia
(C) Iran
(D) Pakistan

Q13 The Opium War of 1839-1842 was fought by the British against which of the following countries?

(A) Afghanistan
(B) China
(C) India
(D) Indochina

Q14 The term "Licensing Raj" refers to which of the following:

(A) Regulation of private businesses in India after independence
(B) Hunting regulations in India during British rule in India
(C) Mercantilist regulations set up by the British East India Company
(D) Education system prior to British rule in India

Q15 Nollywood produces approximately 50 full-length films a week, making it the world's second most prolific film industry after Bollywood in Bombay, India. Which of the following is the city in which Nollywood is based?

(A) Toronto
(B) Nippon
(C) Lagos
(D) Moscow

Q16 The Cancun climate conference which was held in 2010 reached an agreement called REDD. What was the principal objective of REDD?

(A) To reduce carbon dioxide emissions from cars

(B) To reduce carbon dioxide emissions from electricity generation

(C) To reduce the pace worldwide of forest loss

(D) To transfer resources (money) from developed countries to less developed countries to combat climate change

Q17 Peter travels from the U.S. to Peru, from Peru to Brazil, and then back to the U.S. He leaves the U.S. with $1,000, which he converts into Peruvian Soles at a rate of PS 8/ USD. While in Peru, he spends 3,200 Soles. Then, he converted the remaining Soles into Cruzeiros at a rate of PS 1.2 / BC. He spends 2,000 Cruzeiros. Finally, he converts any remaining Cruzeiros into USD upon his return to the US at a rate of BC 5 / USD. How many US Dollars did he spend during his trip?

(A) $248
(B) $400
(C) $600
(D) $752

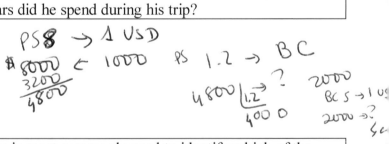

Q18 The Middle Kingdom is most commonly used to identify which of the following countries?

(A) China
(B) United Kingdom
(C) Saudi Arabia
(D) Belgium

Q19 The League of Nations was established at the Treaty of Versailles after the end of the first World War. The creation of the League of Nations was a centerpiece of President Woodrow Wilson's Fourteen Points for Peace. Which of the following countries was never a member of the League of Nations?

(A) China
(B) United States
(C) Germany
(D) Japan

Q20 Which of the following is the oldest city in the U.S. that was founded by European settlers?

(A) St. Augustine, FL
(B) Santa Fe, NM
(C) Los Angeles, CA
(D) El Paso, TX

Q21 Which of the following events is known as the trail of tears?

(A) The forced marches that concentration camp detainees were forced to take at the end of World War II

(B) The trip that Cherokee Indians were forced to take from Georgia to Oklahoma

(C) The return of escaped African Americans slaves from northern states to the South

(D) The route that the Mormons took when they resettled in Utah after the murder of Joseph Smith in Illinois

Q22 The Seneca Falls Declaration of Sentiments and Resolutions called for better (or more equal) treatment of which of the following?

(A) African Americans
(B) Women
(C) Native Americans
(D) Mexican Americans

Q23 The term "AAMOF" is most likely to mean which of the following?

    (A)   An international trade organization
    (B)   African-American Movement of Freedom
    (C)   As a matter of fact
    (D)   A treaty between the U.S. and Russia

Q24 Which of the following Asian country was formerly known as Ceylon?

    (A)   Cambodia
    (B)   Sri Lanka
    (C)   Thailand
    (D)   Myanmar

Q25 In 2007, a country announced the discovery of oil deposits in a field deep below the seabed off its coast. This is oil field has become the largest oil discovery in recent times. In which country is this field located?

    (A)   Brazil
    (B)   Norway
    (C)   Canada
    (D)   Venezuela

Q26 Which of the following countries is most likely to be classified as a Baltic country?

    (A)   Norway
    (B)   Croatia
    (C)   Romania
    (D)   Latvia

Q27 Which country hosted military bases of both the United States and Russia in the 2000s?

    (A)   Ukraine
    (B)   Kyrgyzstan
    (C)   Macedonia
    (D)   Afghanistan

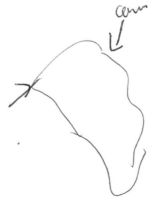

Q28 Which of the following countries best fits this description?
Country located in Central America with its North Coast on the Caribbean
Sea and the South Coast on the Pacific Ocean. This country was
originally settled by the Mayans, and Columbus discovered it for the
Europeans in 1502. The country's name is derived from a name given to
the area by Columbus. U.S. companies owned vast banana plantations on
this country's North Coast during the 20th Century, and this country
hosted one of the largest Peace Corps delegations in the world.

(A) Panama
(B) Dominican Republic
(C) Honduras
(D) Costa Rica

Q29 All Western European countries that are members of the EU adopted the
Euro currency except for three countries. Three of the four countries
listed below have not adopted the Euro. Please select the country that
HAS adopted the Euro as its currency from the following list:

(A) United Kingdom
(B) Sweden
(C) Finland
(D) Denmark

Q30 If the extension at the end of a file name is .htm, what is this file most
likely to have?

(A) An image
(B) An executable file
(C) An application
(D) A web page

Q31 Which of the following is the best example of a Pigouvian tax?

(A) A tax on cigarettes
(B) A tax rate that increases as incomes increase
(C) A value-added tax
(D) A property tax

Q32 The Age Discrimination Act of 1967 protects employees ages _____ and above from age discrimination.

    (A) 40

    (B) 50

    (C) 55

    (D) 60

Q33 What is the median of the following numbers: -5, -2, 8, 12, 14, 14, 18, 21

    (A) 10

    (B) 13

    (C) 14

    (D) 26

Q34 Mercosur is a trade block among countries from which of the following regions:

    (A) South East Asia

    (B) South America

    (C) Sub-Saharan Africa

    (D) Balkans

Q35 The Treaty on Open Skies is most likely to deal with which of the following?

    (A) Increase in the number of air routes between participant countries

    (B) A regime of unarmed aerial observation over the territory of its participants

    (C) A program for space exploration

    (D) Rules to increase competition on commercial air routes among participant countries

Q36 Many interstate highways in the U.S. have (or had until the 1990s) a maximum speed limit of 55 miles per hour. What is the reason for that speed limit?

(A) To reduce gasoline consumption
(B) To reduce the number of accidental deaths and serious injuries
(C) Because cars in the 1940s and 1950s could not safely drive at higher speeds.
(D) To reduce the rate of accidents among young people

Q37 The term "START" is most likely to mean which of the following?

(A) Standard terminal access – Refresh task
(B) A congressional office that conducts research for members of Congress
(C) A database software
(D) A treaty signed between the United States and the Soviet Union that aimed to reduce the number of nuclear weapons

Q38 Where was the first Ferris Wheel located?

(A) London, next to the Thames River
(B) Chicago for the World's Fair
(C) Coney Island at an amusement park
(D) San Francisco

Q39 The Temperance movement was most concerned with which of the following?

(A) Smoking
(B) Slavery
(C) Alcohol
(D) Voting rights

Q40   Who was the first African-American author that published a book?

  (A)   Harriet Beecher Stowe
  (B)   Frederick Douglass
  (C)   Harriet Tubman
  (D)   Phyllis Wheatley

Q41   The price of corn is $10 per bushel. Due to a drought in the mid-west, the price increases by 20%. Subsequently, imports from Brazil increase dramatically to meet the demand for corn and prices decline by 25%. After these two price changes, the price of corn is closest to which of the following?

  (A) $6.00
  (B) $8.00
  (C) $9.00
  (D) $9.50

Q42   In internet advertising, CPC and CPM are most likely to refer to which of the following?

  (A)   Cost per one hundred clicks; Cost per one million clicks
  (B)   Cost per one hundred clicks; Cost per one thousand clicks
  (C)   Cost per click; Cost per one thousand impressions
  (D)   Cost per click; Cost per one million impressions

Q43   Franklin D. Roosevelt was known for his "Fireside Chats". Which of the following did this term refer to?

  (A)   Filmed addresses played in theaters prior to movies
  (B)   Newspaper opinion columns
  (C)   Television address
  (D)   Radio address

Q44   In a presidential election, if none of the candidates receives more than 50% of the electoral college votes, what happens?

    (A)   The candidate with the most electoral votes becomes president

    (B)   The Senate decides who becomes president

    (C)   The House of Representatives decides who becomes president, with each state having one vote

    (D)   Congress (both houses) decides who becomes president, with each member of each of the houses having one vote

Q45   In which of the following places did George Washington surrender to the enemy?

    (A)   Saratoga
    (B)   Trenton
    (C)   Ft. Necessity
    (D)   Valley Forge

Q46   The Declaration of Independence states that governments derive their power from the consent of the governed, and that the people have a right to change their government. This theory is best described as:

    (A)   Democracy
    (B)   Social Compact
    (C)   Republicanism
    (D)   Political legitimacy

Q47   Which of the following approvals is required for a constitutional amendment to be ratified?

    (A)   Three fourths of the state legislatures
    (B)   Three fourths of both houses of Congress
    (C)   Two thirds of the state legislatures
    (D)   Two thirds of both houses of Congress

propose 2/3

Q48　Which of the following is known as Secretary of State Seward's Folly?

(A)　The decision to build the Panama Canal in 1881

(B)　The Alaska purchase of 1867

(C)　The attack on the Hawaiian Islands and U.S. support for Queen Lili'uokalani

(D)　The actions that led to the United States and the United Kingdom almost engaging in military action in Canada

Q49　Sutter's Mill is best known for which of the following?

(A)　The first mill built in the US, which started the American Industrial Revolution

(B)　The machine that helped separate the cotton's fibers from its seeds

(C)　The largest and most important British textile manufacturing plant during the First Industrial Revolution

(D)　The place where gold was first discovered in California

Q50　In the late 19th Century, a new form of entertainment grew out of minstrel shows and became popular with American families by including dancing, singing, juggling, animals and other acts. Which of the following best describes this form of entertainment?

(A)　Burlesque
(B)　Circus
(C)　Revue
(D)　Vaudeville

Q51　When a Chinese person responds to a request with "maybe" or "we'll see", he is most likely to mean which of the following?

(A)　Yes
(B)　No
(C)　I need to think about it and will get back to you.
(D)　I need to ask my superiors.

Q52   Which of the following Supreme Court cases upheld the Jim Crow laws by creating the "separate but equal" doctrine?

- (A)   Brown v. Board of Education
- (B)   Plessy v. Ferguson
- (C)   Marbury v. Madison
- (D)   Dred Scott v. Sanford

Q53   Which of the following economic theories believes that government should not interfere in the economy during cyclical booms and busts because the market will self-correct without the need of government intervention?

- (A)   Supply-side economics
- (B)   Classical economics
- (C)   Keynesian economics
- (D)   Smithian economics

Q54   How many electoral college votes are there in a US presidential election?

- (A)   434
- (B)   535
- (C)   536
- (D)   538

Q55   The interest rate at which the Federal Reserve lends to member banks is called:

- (A)   The Discount rate
- (B)   The Federal Funds rate
- (C)   The LIBOR rate
- (D)   The Treasury rate

Q56   Shield laws have been established to provide protection to which of the following:

- (A)   Racial minorities
- (B)   Whistle blowers
- (C)   Journalists
- (D)   Police

Q57 A reporter is conducting an interview on the record and recording it on tape. After 15 minutes, the source requests that the reporter turn the tape off before providing some additional information on a political candidate. After providing this information, the reporter turns the recorder back on. When writing the story, which of the following is most likely to happen:

(A) The reporter can provide quotes on what the source said during the whole interview, regardless of whether the recorder was on or off.

(B) The reporter can provide quotes on what the source said during the recorded portions of the interview, but can only paraphrase the information given when the recorder was turned off.

(C) The reporter can provide quotes on what the source said during the recorded portions of the interview, but cannot provide any information given while the recorder was turned off.

(D) The reporter can provide quotes of what was said while the recorder was on, but he cannot name the source when paraphrasing information during the portion that was not recorded.

Q58 The Literary Digest conducted a poll to determine who would win the 1936 presidential election, Franklin Roosevelt or Alfred Landon. The magazine collected names from telephone directories and automobile registrations to select a random sample of over two million Americans. Based on polling this large sample, the magazine erroneously predicted an overwhelming victory for Landon. Which of the following is the most likely explanation for this mistake?

(A) Random error
(B) Data mining
(C) Sample selection bias
(D) Placebo effect

Q59 If a country has a primary deficit, this is most likely to mean that:

(A) The government's revenues are less than the government expenses, using Purchasing Power Parity foreign exchange rates

(B) The government's revenues are less than the government expenses, excluding energy imports

(C) The government's revenues are less than the government expenses, excluding interest expenses

(D) The government's revenues are less than the government expenses, excluding foreign exchange losses

Q60 Pirates based in Somalia are most likely to attack vessels traveling through which of the following:

(A) Gulf of Aden
(B) Persian Gulf
(C) Strait of Malacca
(D) Strait of Hormuz

Answers

Q1 C George Kennan wrote the "Long Telegram", which was a basis for the policy of containment. Kennan died in 2005 at age 101. His authorized biography was published by John Gaddis in 2011.

Q2 A Iraq. The cradle of civilization is a term that usually refers to the Fertile Crescent in Mesopotamia (Tigris and Euphrates rivers), in the Middle East. The civilization of Sumer, located in present-day Iraq, was the first civilization with a written language.

Q3 B The railroads.

Q4 B Libya was the first country to achieve independence in 1951 through the United Nations, and has the largest oil reserves in Africa.

Q5 D The fire at the Triangle Shirtwaist factory on March 25th 1911 killed 146 people, mostly immigrant women. This tragedy became the catalyst for major reforms in public-safety codes and led to the New Deal's labor legislation of the 1930s.

Q6 B Shinto is the indigenous religion of Japan ("When the Catfish stirs" The Economist 7/2/09). There were many articles written about Japan's culture during the earthquake of 2011.

Q7 A Research in Motion (RIM) is a Canadian company that produces the Blackberry smart phone. In 2013, RIM announced that it would change the company's name to Blackberry.

Q8 D Libya has the largest proved oil reserves in Africa (48.1 billion barrels in 2011). Libya had the ninth largest oil reserves in the world after Russia, and the largest in Africa; the second largest are in Nigeria (38.5 billion barrels). Source: CIA World Factbook (2013).

Q9 B Egypt is the most populous Arab country with 79 million people (2010). Indonesia is not an Arab country, even though it is more populous than Egypt, with over 200 million inhabitants.

Q10 D Cloud computing is Internet-based computing, whereby shared resources, software, and information are provided to computers and other devices on demand, like the electricity grid. (Wikipedia)

Q11 **C** Circulation at the Wall Street Journal was over 2 million during the latest six-month reporting period, surpassing the second-largest newspaper, USA Todays with a daily circulation of 1.8 million.

Q12 **A** Indonesia has the largest Muslim population in the world, approximately 200 million, followed by Pakistan and India.

Q13 **B** The Opium War was a war between Britain and China. The Opium War was not only about opium, but also about free trade. As a result of the war, China ceded Hong Kong island to Britain.

Q14 **A** The term Licensing Raj is used to describe the elaborate licenses, regulations and accompanying red tape that were required to set up and run businesses in India between 1947 and 1990. President Obama referred to the licensing Raj during a speech during his 2010 visit to India (WSJ, 11/09/2010)

Q15 **C** Nollywood is based in Lagos, Nigeria. (Economist 12/18/2010)

Q16 **C** REDD (Reducing Emissions from Deforestation and Forest Degradation) is an agreement to reward countries for lowering rates of deforestation (Economist 12/18/2010).

Q17 **C** The correct answer is $600.

First step: convert $1,000 into PS 8,000 (by multiplying by 8).

Second step: Spend PS 3,200 – remaining cash PS 4,800

Third step: Convert PS 4,800 into BC 4,000 (by dividing by 1.2). There are 1.2 Soles for each Cruzeiro – so Peter will have fewer Cruzeiros than Soles.

Fourth Step: Spend BC 2,000. He has BC 2,000 left.

Fifth Step: Convert BC 2,000 into $400.

Sixth Step: Because he has $400 left, and he started out with $1,000, he spent $600.

(This question is a little more complicated than those you will likely encounter in the exam. However, if you learn how to answer this question, you will be ready for any similar questions).

Q18 **A** Middle Kingdom is a term that refers to China.

Q19 B President Woodrow Wilson received the Nobel Peace Prize for his efforts to promote and establish the League of Nations. However, the U.S. Senate did not ratify the Treaty of Versailles and the United States never became a member of the League of Nations.

Q20 A The oldest city in the U.S. is St. Augustine, FL. It was founded in 1565, approximately 20 years before English explorers arrived to the island of Roanoke.

Q21 B The Trail of Tears refers to the forced resettlement of the Cherokee Indians of Georgia to Oklahoma. 25% of the approximately 15,000 Cherokees that took the trip died in the Trail of Tears.

Q22 B The Seneca Falls Declaration of Sentiments and Resolutions of 1948 was led by Elizabeth Cady Stanton and Lucretia Mott, and called for equality for women, such as equal employment and the right to vote.

Q23 C AAMOF is a common abbreviation that stands for "as a matter of fact".

(These abbreviations fall under the topics of communications and computers, and may be tested in the exam. We provide a list of common abbreviations in the last pages of the book.)

Q24 B Sri Lanka, an island state off the cost of India, was known as Ceylon until 1972.

Q25 A Petrobras announced in November 2007 that it had made the biggest discovery of oil of this century. The Santos Basin is a 136,008 sq. miles offshore pre salt basin located in the south Atlantic ocean 190 mi south east of São Paulo, Brazil. One of the largest Brazilian sedimentary basins, it is the site of several recent (2007-2008) significant oil fields, including Tupi and Jupiter.

Q26 D The Baltic Sea is located in Northern Europe. The following countries border on this inland sea: Denmark, Estonia, Finland, Germany, Latvia, Lithuania, Poland, Russia and Sweden. The Baltic States is a term that refers to Estonia, Latvia and Lithuania. In early 2009, the government of Latvia fell after the IMF imposed austerity measures and S&P downgraded the country's debt to junk. The Baltic states are members of the European Union.

Q27 B Kyrgyzstan is the only country that hosted both Americana and Russian military bases during the war in Afghanistan.

Q28 C Honduras is the only country that matches the description above. Panama was not discovered by Columbus. The Dominican Republic is in a Caribbean Island and does not have a coast on the Pacific Ocean. Costa Rica was not named by Columbus and was not settled by the Mayans.

Q29 C As of 2009, the euro (€) is the official currency of 16 of the 27 member states of the European Union (EU). These countries are known as the Eurozone, and include: Austria, Belgium, Cyprus, Finland, France, Germany, Greece, Ireland, Italy, Luxembourg, Malta, the Netherlands, Portugal, Slovakia, Slovenia and Spain.

Q30 D .htm and .html files are web pages. HTM stands for Hypertext Markup Language, which is used to develop web pages.

Q31 A A Pigouvian tax is named after Arthur Pigou, a 20th Century British economist. Pigouvian taxes are imposed on goods whose price does not reflect the true total social cost of their consumption. Typical examples include taxes on cigarettes, alcohol or gambling. Recently there have been discussions about Pigouvian taxes on non-diet sodas and fast food.

Q32 A Age discrimination protection applies to employees age 40 and above.

Q33 B The median is 13 (the middle value). Because there are an even number of values, we take the two middle values (12 and 14) and average them, getting 13. The mean (or average) is 10. The mode is 14. The range is 26.

Q34 B Mercosur or Mercosul is a Regional Trade Agreement founded in 1991 by Argentina, Brazil, Paraguay and Uruguay, countries located in South America.

Q35 B The Treaty of Open Skies entered into force in 2002 and currently has 34 parties. The Treaty establishes a regime of unarmed aerial observation over the entire territory of its participants. The Treaty is designed to enhance mutual understanding and confidence by giving all participants, regardless of size, a direct role in gathering information about military forces and activities of concern to them.

Do not confuse the Treaty of Open Skies with the Open Skies Agreement that liberalized trans-Atlantic air travel.

Q36 A The national speed limit of 55 MPH attempted to conserve energy as a response to the oil price spikes and supply disruptions during the 1973 oil crisis.

Q37 D The United States and the former Soviet Union signed the START Treaty (Strategic Arms Reduction Treaty) in 1991 to remove thousands of nuclear warheads from their operational forces.

Q38 B The first Ferris Wheel was built by George Ferris in 1893 for the World's Fair in Chicago

Q39 C The temperance movement was concerned with alcoholism and with reducing (or eliminating) the consumption of alcohol. Ultimately, the 18th amendment to the constitution prohibited alcohol consumption in the U.S.

Q40 D Phyllis Wheatley was the first African-American to publish a poem book in 1773. Phyllis Wheatley was a slave that gained her freedom after the book's publication.

Q41 C The price of corn first increased from $10 to $12 ($10 * 1.2 = $12). Subsequently, the price of corn declined by $3, or 25% of $12 ($12 * 0.25 = $3), to $9 ($12 - $3 = $9).

Q42 C CPC: Cost per click
CPM: Cost per one thousand impressions (M is 1,000 in Roman numerals)

Q43 D Fireside chats were a series of radio addresses given by President Franklin D. Roosevelt to address the nation.

Q44 C The candidate that receives the most votes in the electoral college becomes president, only if the candidate receives more than 50% of the votes. If no one receives more than 50% of the votes, the House of Representatives elects the president, with each state having one vote. In the 1824 elections neither candidate received 50% of the votes and the election was decided in the House of Representatives. John Quincy Adams became president even though Andrew Jackson had received a greater number of electoral college votes. This episode became known as the Corrupt Bargain after Henry Clay, the Speaker of the House, became Secretary of State under John Quincy Adams.

Q45 C George Washington was a British officer during the French and Indian War. In 1754 George Washington surrendered Ft. Necessity to the French.

Q46 B The Social Compact or Social Contract is a theory of government that states that governments derive their political authority from the consent of the governed.

Q47 A An amendment can be proposed by two thirds vote of both houses of Congress. An amendment needs to be ratified by three-fourths of the state legislatures or by conventions in three fourths of the states.

Q48 B The purchase of Alaska was known as Seward's Folly. William Seward was Governor of New York and Secretary of State under Presidents Lincoln and Johnson.

Q49 D In 1848, gold was discovered at Sutter's Mill near Sacramento, California. This discovery started the California Gold Rush. The first mill (textile manufacturing plant) was built by Samuel Slater, a British immigrant to the US. Slater built the first mill (Slater's Mill) in the late 18th Century in Rhode Island. The cotton gin was the machine that helped revolutionize the cotton industry in the U.S. by allowing people to quickly remove the seeds from the cotton fibers.

Q50 D Vaudeville became popular with families in the late 19th Century by combining acts from musicians, acrobats and magicians, such as Harry Houdini.

Q51 B Chinese people have difficulty saying no. Instead, they may say "maybe" or "we'll see" when they mean to say "no". (see www.ediplomat.com for more information on cultural etiquette)

Q52 **B** Plessy v. Ferguson established the "separate but equal" doctrine in 1896. Brown v. Board of Education (1954) stated that separate but equal has no place because separate facilities are "inherently unequal". Marbury v. Madison (1803) established the principle of judicial review. Dred Scott v. Sanford (1857) determined that African Americans were not citizens.

Q53 **B** Classical economics are based on Adam Smith's book The Wealth of Nations, in which he presented the view that the invisible hand of the markets will help markets adjust in response to the market cycles without need of government intervention.

Q54 **D** There are 538 votes in the electoral college. Each state gets a number of electoral votes equal to its representation in Congress (2 for senators + number of representatives). There are 100 senators and 435 representatives for a total of 535. In addition, the District of Columbia gets 3 electoral college votes as required by the 23rd amendment to the Constitution. Thus, the total of electoral votes is 538 (535 for the 50 states and 3 for the District of Columbia).

Q55 **A** The Discount rate is the rate at which the Federal reserve lends money to banks. The Federal Funds rate is the rate at which banks lend to each other in the overnight market to meet their reserve requirements. The LIBOR rate is a rate at which banks lend to each other. The Treasury rate is a rate at which the US Treasury borrows money.

Q56 **C** Shield laws provide protection to journalists by protecting them against requirements to disclose their sources. In a 2005 case reporter Judith Miller of the New York Times spent almost three months in jail for refusing to disclose her sources on a story in which she publicly released the name of CIA officer Valerie Plame.

Q57 **A** Unless the source requested that the interview be off-the-record or on background, the reporter can quote anything said during the interview, whether the recorder was on or off. The reporter can write notes while the interviewee speaks, so that he can accurately quote him in the article.

Q58 **C** The selection of random names from vehicle registrations and phone directories may be appropriate today. In the 1930's depression, only the more affluent people were able to afford these items. Thus, the sample, though large at two million, was more affluent than the overall population. As a result, the poll resulted in the wrong prediction due to sample bias. Sample bias occurs when a segment of the population is over-represented compared to other segments. For example, if one conducted a poll of readers of Cosmopolitan magazine, the sample bias would be that there would likely be more women than men in the sample.

Q59 C A primary budget deficit means that the government's revenues (e.g., tax collections) exceed the government's expenses, excluding interest costs.

Q60 A Pirates based in Somalia are known to attack ships traveling in the Indian Ocean, usually in the Gulf of Aden located between Somalia and Yemen.

Biographical Information Test

We recommend that you take this test under the same constraints you will have in the exam. Take the whole test within 40 minutes, without bathroom breaks. You have an average of 32 seconds per question (75 questions). Try to write as many examples as possible in those questions that request examples.

You may notice that some questions are similar. The Department of State will include some questions that are similar to check for consistency of responses. After you finish the test check your answers for consistency.

Q1	Did you graduate from college with any honors? Which?

- (A) None
- (B) Cum Laude
- (C) Magna Cum Laude
- (D) Summa Cum Laude
- (E) Other

(If you answered E, please explain)

_____

_____

_____

_____

Q2	How persuasive would your supervisors, teachers or colleagues say you are when making an argument or a proposal?

- (A) Much more persuasive than other people
- (B) Somewhat more persuasive than other people
- (C) About as persuasive as other people
- (D) Somewhat less persuasive than other people
- (E) Not persuasive at all

Q3	When you make a presentation in front of a large group of people, how likely are to feel anxious before or during the presentation?

- (A) Very much
- (B) Much
- (C) Some
- (D) A little
- (E) Very little

Q4	During the last three years, how many times have you spoken in front of a large group of people (i.e., 10 or more)?

- (A) 0
- (B) 1
- (C) 2
- (D) 3
- (E) 4 or more

(If you answered C, D or E, list the topics of the discussions)

_____

_____

_____

Q5   How many books have you read in the last 6 months?

    (A)   0
    (B)   1
    (C)   2
    (D)   3
    (E)   4 or more

(If you answered B, C, D or E, list the books)

_____

_____

_____

_____

Q6   How many friends do you have that are not of your ethnic background?

    (A)   0
    (B)   1
    (C)   2
    (D)   3
    (E)   4 or more

Q7   How many positions of leadership did you hold in high school?

    (A)   0
    (B)   1
    (C)   2
    (D)   3
    (E)   4 or more

(If you answered B, C, D or E, list examples)

_____

_____

_____

_____

Q8   How many letters have you written to newspaper/magazine editors?

    (A)   0
    (B)   1
    (C)   2
    (D)   3
    (E)   4 or more

Q9   How many letters that you have written to newspaper/magazine editors were published?

    (A)   0
    (B)   1
    (C)   2
    (D)   3
    (E)   4 or more

(If you answered B, C, D or E, list the topics of the letters and publications in which they appeared)

_____

_____

_____

_____

Q10   How many countries have you visited in the last 24 months? *2 years*

    (A)   0
    (B)   1
    (C)   2
    (D)   3
    (E)   4 or more

Q11   How many countries have you visited or lived in for more than 30 contiguous days?

    (A)   0
    (B)   1
    (C)   2
    (D)   3
    (E)   4 or more

(If you answered B, C, D or E, list the countries)

France   Switzerland
Rwanda
DRC
Canada

Q12   How comfortable are you starting a conversation with a person you do not know?

    (A)   Much more comfortable than other people
    (B)   Somewhat more comfortable than other people
    (C)   About as comfortable as other people
    (D)   Somewhat less comfortable than other people
    (E)   Not comfortable at all

Q13   How many museums or art exhibits have you visited in the last 12 months?

    (A)   0
    (B)   1
    (C)   2
    (D)   3
    (E)   4 or more

(If you answered B, C, D or E, list the museums)

MOK African American Museum DC

Q14   How many periodicals (e.g., magazines, newspapers) do you read on a regular basis?

    (A)   0
    (B)   1
    (C)   2
    (D)   3
    (E)   4 or more

(If you answered B, C, D or E, list the periodicals)

NYT, the Economist,
La lettre du Continent

Q15   How many books have you read in the last 12 months that deal with cultures different than your own?

    (A)   0
    (B)   1
    (C)   2
    (D)   3
    (E)   4 or more

Q16   How often do you come up with solutions that are "outside the box"?

    (A)   Very often
    (B)   Often
    (C)   Sometimes
    (D)   Seldom
    (E)   Never

Q17   How many events attended by more than 10 people have you organized in the last 12 months?

    (A)   0
    (B)   1
    (C)   2
    (D)   3
    (E)   4 or more

(If you answered B, C, D or E, list the events)

_____

_____

_____

_____

Q18   How often do you write memos, articles or other materials that are at least five pages long?

    (A)   Very often
    (B)   Often
    (C)   Sometimes
    (D)   Seldom
    (E)   Never

Q19 How many leadership positions have you held in nonprofit or other volunteer organizations?

    (A)   0
    (B)   1
    (C)   2
    (D)   3
    (E)   4 or more

(If you answered B, C, D or E, list the position and type of organization)

_____

_____

_____

_____

Q20 How likely are you to offer to take additional responsibilities at work or at school?

    (A)   Much more likely than other people
    (B)   Somewhat more likely than other people
    (C)   About as likely as other people
    (D)   Somewhat less likely than other people
    (E)   Much less likely than other people

Q21 How often do your colleagues ask you for help when they are having difficulties with their work?

    (A)   Very often
    (B)   Often
    (C)   Sometimes
    (D)   Seldom
    (E)   Never

Q22 How many friends do you have whose first language is not English?

    (A)   0
    (B)   1
    (C)   2
    (D)   3
    (E)   4 or more

(If you answered B, C, D or E, list the languages)

_____

_____

_____

Q23   How often do your seek advise from your colleagues at work?

    (A)   Very often
    (B)   Often
    (C)   Sometimes
    (D)   Seldom
    (E)   Never

Q24   How likely would your supervisors, teachers or colleagues say that you are at asking questions during the Q&A part of a presentation or meeting?

    (A)   Much more likely than other people
    (B)   Somewhat more likely than other people
    (C)   About as likely as other people
    (D)   Somewhat less likely than other people
    (E)   Much less likely than other people

Q25   How would you rate your writing style?

    (A)   Much better than that of other people
    (B)   Somewhat better than that of other people
    (C)   About as good as that of other people
    (D)   Somewhat worse than that of other people
    (E)   Much worse than that of other people

Q26   How often do you participate in events in which you do not know other people?

    (A)   Very often
    (B)   Often
    (C)   Sometimes
    (D)   Seldom
    (E)   Never

Q27   How often do you send a written thank you note to show appreciation for a present, a favor or something else?

    (A)   Very often
    (B)   Often
    (C)   Sometimes
    (D)   Seldom
    (E)   Never

Q28   How many concerts have you attended in the last 12 months

    (A)   0
    (B)   1
    (C)   2
    (D)   3
    (E)   4 or more

(If you answered B, C, D or E, list the concerts)

_____

_____

_____

_____

Q29   How good would your friends and relatives say that you are at selecting gifts?

    (A)   Much better than other people
    (B)   Somewhat better than other people
    (C)   About as good as other people
    (D)   Somewhat worse than other people
    (E)   Much worse than other people

Q30   In the last six months, how many times did you offer or volunteer to help with a task that is beyond your principal responsibilities?

    (A)   0
    (B)   1
    (C)   2
    (D)   3
    (E)   4 or more

(If you answered B, C, D or E, list examples)

_____

_____

_____

_____

Q31   How many positions of leadership did you hold in college?

    (A)   0
    (B)   1
    (C)   2
    (D)   3
    (E)   4 or more

(If you answered B, C, D or E, list examples)

International Student Association

_____

_____

_____

Q32   How many countries did you visit for work or study?

    (A)   0
    (B)   1
    (C)   2
    (D)   3
    (E)   4 or more

(If you answered B, C, D or E, list examples)

_____

_____

_____

_____

Q33   How trusting would your supervisors, teachers or colleagues say that you are?

    (A)   Much more trusting than other people
    (B)   Somewhat more trusting than other people
    (C)   About as trusting as other people
    (D)   Somewhat less trusting than other people
    (E)   Much less trusting than other people

Q34   How many of your jobs or volunteer positions require you to organize events attended by more than 10 people?

   (A) 0
   (B) 1
   (C) 2
   (D) 3
   (E) 4 or more

(If you answered B, C, D or E, list examples)

_____

_____

_____

_____

Q35   How would your supervisors, teachers or colleagues describe you?

   (A) Much more self-confident than he should be
   (B) Somewhat more self-confident than he should be
   (C) Appropriately confident
   (D) Somewhat less self-confident than he should be
   (E) Much less self-confident than he should be

Q36   In the last six months, how many times did you offer or volunteer to help with a task that is menial or underappreciated?

   (A) 0
   (B) 1
   (C) 2
   (D) 3
   (E) 4 or more

(If you answered B, C, D or E, list examples)

_____

_____

_____

Q37   How comfortable are you interacting with members of other ethnic groups?

   (A) Much more comfortable than other people
   (B) Somewhat more comfortable than other people
   (C) About as comfortable as other people
   (D) Somewhat less comfortable than other people
   (E) Much less comfortable than other people

Q38   How many hobbies do you engage in a regular basis?

    (A)   0
    (B)   1
    (C)   2
    (D)   3
    (E)   4 or more

Q39   How comfortable would your supervisors, teachers or colleagues say that you are at making presentations in front of more than 10 people?

    (A)   Much more comfortable than other people
    (B)   Somewhat more comfortable than other people
    (C)   About as comfortable as other people
    (D)   Somewhat less comfortable than other people
    (E)   Much less comfortable than other people

Q40   How often do your colleagues ask you for help with personal issues unrelated to work?

    (A)   Very often
    (B)   Often
    (C)   Sometimes
    (D)   Seldom
    (E)   Never

Q41   How many board games do you play on a regular basis?

    (A)   0
    (B)   1
    (C)   2
    (D)   3
    (E)   4 or more

(If you answered B, C, D or E, list examples)

Checkers _____

_____

_____

_____

Q42   How often do you feel stress before going on a long trip?

    (A)   Very often
    (B)   Often
    (C)   Sometimes
    (D)   Seldom
    (E)   Never

Q43 How effective would your supervisors, teachers or colleagues say that you are at adjusting your recommendations or analysis when you receive new information?

(A) Much more effective than other people
(B) Somewhat more effective than other people
(C) About as effective as other people
(D) Somewhat less effective than other people
(E) Much less effective than other people

Q44 How often do you show interest in people's personal lives?

(A) Very often
(B) Often
(C) Sometimes
(D) Seldom
(E) Never

Q45 How often do you write tasks you need to accomplish in a notebook or agenda?

(A) Very often
(B) Often
(C) Sometimes
(D) Seldom
(E) Never

Q46 How would your supervisors, teachers or colleagues describe your ability to come up with creative ideas or solutions to school or work problems?

(A) Much more creative than other people
(B) Somewhat more creative than other people
(C) About as creative as other people
(D) Somewhat less creative than other people
(E) Much less creative than other people

Q47 How likely are your supervisors, teachers or colleagues to say that you have good judgment when evaluating a problem?

(A) Much more likely than other people
(B) Somewhat more likely than other people
(C) About as likely as other people
(D) Somewhat less likely than other people
(E) Much less likely than other people

Q48   Over the last five years, how many classes or courses (that are not required by your job) have you taken in order to improve your skills?

     (A)   0
     (B)   1
     (C)   2
     (D)   3
     (E)   4 or more

(If you answered B, C, D or E, list examples)

_____

_____

_____

_____

Q49   Over the last 12 months, how many times has a supervisor, teacher or colleague ask you for help with a computer or technology issue?

     (A)   0
     (B)   1
     (C)   2
     (D)   3
     (E)   4 or more

Q50   How many different U.S. states have you lived in for at least 6 consecutive months?

     (A)   1
     (B)   2
     (C)   3
     (D)   4
     (E)   5 or more

(If you answered C, D or E, list examples)

_New Hampshire_____

_Delaware_____

_Maryland_____

_Pennsylvania_____

Q51   How often do people ask you for a recommendation on a book to read or movie to watch?

(A)   Very often
(B)   Often
(C)   Sometimes
(D)   Seldom
(E)   Never

Q52   On average, how many times a month do you go out with friends?

(A)   0
(B)   1-4
(C)   5-8
(D)   9-12
(E)   13 or more

(If you answered B, C, D or E, list the two most common activities)

– Movies
– Amusement/Recreation park for kids

Q53   How impatient would your supervisors, teachers or colleagues say that you are when dealing with colleagues and/or employees that report to you?

(A)   Much more impatient than other people
(B)   Somewhat more impatient than other people
(C)   About as impatient as other people
(D)   Somewhat less impatient than other people
(E)   Much less impatient than other people

Q54   How many times a week do you exercise?

(A)   0
(B)   1
(C)   2
(D)   3
(E)   4 or more

Q55 Over the last 12 months, how many team sports have you played on a regular basis?

(A) 0
(B) 1
(C) 2
(D) 3
(E) 4 or more

(If you answered B, C, D or E, list some examples)

_____

_____

_____

_____

Q56 When preparing a presentation, how often do you prepare by "giving" the presentation out loud by yourself or with a friend?

(A) Very often
(B) Often
(C) Sometimes
(D) Seldom
(E) Never

Q57 How would your supervisors, teachers or colleagues describe your ability to mediate conflicts among co-workers, students, etc.?

(A) Much more capable than other people
(B) Somewhat more capable than other people
(C) About as capable as other people
(D) Somewhat less capable than other people
(E) Much less capable than other people

Q58 How many books have you read in the last 12 months?

(A) 0
(B) 1
(C) 2
(D) 3
(E) 4 or more

(If you answered B, C, D or E, list the books)

_____

_____

_____

Q59 How effective would your supervisors, teachers or colleagues say that you are at using appropriate humor at work or school?

    (A)   Much more effective than other people
    (B)   Somewhat more effective than other people
    (C)   About as effective as other people
    (D)   Somewhat less effective than other people
    (E)   Much less effective than other people

Q60 How many different languages do you speak conversationally?

    (A)   0
    (B)   1
    (C)   2
    (D)   3
    (E)   4 or more

(If you answered B, C, D or E, list the languages)

French / English
Djauma
Mina/Ewe

Q61 How would you rate your desire to learn new skills or improve existing skills?

    (A)   Much more than other people
    (B)   Somewhat more than other people
    (C)   About as much as other people
    (D)   Somewhat less than other people
    (E)   Much less than other people

(If you answered A or B, list some of the skills you have tried to learn or improve in the last 12 months)

Q62   How often do you read articles or books about science and technology?

    (A)   Very often
    (B)   Often
    (C)   Sometimes
    (D)   Seldom
    (E)   Never

Q63   How often do your supervisors, teachers or colleagues ask you for advice on technology purchases or help with technology issues?

    (A)   Very often
    (B)   Often
    (C)   Sometimes
    (D)   Seldom
    (E)   Never

Q64   How fast do you usually drive on the highway?

    (A)   Below the speed limit
    (B)   Up to 5 miles above the speed limit
    (C)   6-10 miles above the speed limit
    (D)   11-20 miles above the speed limit
    (E)   More than 20 miles above the speed limit

Q65   How would your rate your ability in mathematics?

    (A)   Much more capable than other people
    (B)   Somewhat more capable than other people
    (C)   About as capable as other people
    (D)   Somewhat less capable than other people
    (E)   Much less capable than other people

Q66   How would your supervisors, teachers or colleagues describe your ability to clearly and simply explain complex facts or issues?

    (A)   Much more capable than other people
    (B)   Somewhat more capable than other people
    (C)   About as capable as other people
    (D)   Somewhat less capable than other people
    (E)   Much less capable than other people

Q67   How many non-work related leadership positions have you held over the last 12 months?

    (A)   0
    (B)   1
    (C)   2
    (D)   3
    (E)   4 or more

(If you answered B, C, D or E, list your role and the type of entity in which you held the leadership position)

_____

_____

_____

_____

Q68   How many of the positions listed below did you have during educational career (including high school, college and graduate education)?
List: teaching assistant, student council, work-study program, resident advisor or assistant, varsity team)

    (A)   0
    (B)   1
    (C)   2
    (D)   3
    (E)   4 or more

(If you answered B, C, D or E, list the positions)

_____

_____

_____

_____

Q69   How would your supervisors, teachers or colleagues describe your ability to think outside the box?

    (A)   Much more capable than other people
    (B)   Somewhat more capable than other people
    (C)   About as capable as other people
    (D)   Somewhat less capable than other people
    (E)   Much less capable than other people

Q70   How many awards have you received in the last 36 months?

     (A)   0
     (B)   1
     (C)   2
     (D)   3
     (E)   4 or more

(If you answered B, C, D or E, list or describe the awards)

_____

_____

_____

_____

Q71   When you read the newspaper, which of the following sections do you spend more time reading?

     (A)   Business
     (B)   International news
     (C)   National news
     (D)   Opinion/editorial
     (E)   Sports

Q72   How many nonfiction books have you read in the last 12 months?

     (A)   0
     (B)   1
     (C)   2
     (D)   3
     (E)   4 or more

(If you answered B, C, D or E, list the books or topics of the books)

_____

_____

_____

Q73   How frequently do you remember the birthdays of friends, relatives and colleagues and send them an email, card or otherwise wish them a happy birthday?

     (A)   Almost always
     (B)   Often
     (C)   Sometimes
     (D)   Seldom
     (E)   Never

Q74   How likely are you to keep in touch with colleagues from previous jobs or with college classmates?

    (A)   Much more likely than other people
    (B)   Somewhat more likely than other people
    (C)   About as likely as other people
    (D)   Somewhat less likely than other people
    (E)   Much less likely than other people

Q75   How often do your coworkers or classmates ask you to review their work or seek your advice on how to improve their work?

    (A)   Very often
    (B)   Often
    (C)   Sometimes
    (D)   Seldom
    (E)   Never

Chapter VI

Practice Essays

Sample Essays

Answer the first few essays in 45 minutes, and then reduce the amount of time allocated to each essay until you are able to answer the essays in 25 minutes. Write the essays in a computer with the spell check feature turned off. In Microsoft Word, you should click on "file". A menu will open and you should click on "options". A new window will open with the title "Word Options". On the menu on the left, click on "Proofing", and make sure none of the spelling boxes are clicked on (see picture below). This will turn the auto-spell check off.

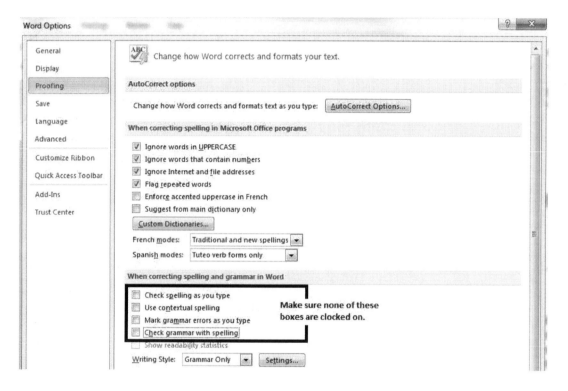

The first eight sample essay prompts are from
http://fsot.wikidot.com/essay.

Essay 11 was provided by the Department of State during an FSOT information session.

Essay 1:
In today's political environment, we have seen the emergence of popular entertainers – singers, musicians, movie stars, and so on – taking center stage to promote and raise money for the candidates of their choice. Some people feel that these entertainers should stick to their own business, while others believe that they have a right, and perhaps even an obligation, to speak their minds. In your view, what do you think the role of entertainers should be in politics? Do they exert undue influence because of their popularity and easy access to the media? Carefully explain the rationale for your position.

Essay 2:
There are numerous viewpoints on the subject of cloning. One side feels that the long-term benefits of cloning – primarily a search for medical cures – is worth the effort, but with some restrictions. Others argue that there is a strong potential for abuse in this era of corporate corruption, dishonesty, and misunderstanding. In your view, aside from religious and moral considerations, who should best make the determination whether cloning is legalized: doctors, politicians, or religious leaders? Carefully explain the rationale for your position.

Essay 3:
The debate over nuclear energy is heating up. Warm winters, and dire warnings by scientists about climate change, have convinced many that carbon emissions might be a bigger danger than nuclear accidents or radioactive waste. Cleaner alternatives such as natural gas and wind exist, but they are more expensive to produce, and supplies can be erratic (in the case of wind) or dependent on unscrupulous suppliers (in the case of natural gas). In your opinion, do the benefits of nuclear energy outweigh its risks? Should power companies invest more in nuclear energy? Carefully explain the rationale for your position.

Essay 4:
America is being reshaped by a wave of immigration. Some say the newcomers cost native workers jobs and depress wages; others say immigrants fill labor shortages and promote new business. The issue is particularly divisive in California and the south-west, where many Mexican migrants work illegally. The failure of America's legal immigration system to attract talented foreigners has also stirred a debate on the need for reform. In your opinion, is immigration reform necessary? Why or why not? Carefully explain the rationale for your position.

Essay 5:
In recent years, many US businesses have begun outsourcing their production overseas. Proponents of this practice argue that cheaper labor abroad translates into lower prices for consumers at home. Their opponents point out that by sending jobs overseas, companies are denying employment to deserving Americans. In your view, is outsourcing beneficial or detrimental to the US economy and American workers? Carefully explain the rationale for your position.

Essay 6:
Government support of the visual and performing arts is at times controversial. Some argue that there should be no government support of the arts but that market forces and patrons should solely support the arts. Others think some government support should be provided but only under the condition that the art presented is judged acceptable by community standards. Still others, however, argue that the arts play an important role in society and should be supported by government funding without any restrictions or conditions. In your view, what should public policy be in regard to supporting the arts? Carefully explain the rationale for your position.

Essay 7:
There is good reason to question the death penalty. A study published in June 2000 showed high rates of error in its use. The judicial system often mishandles capital cases, and minorities fare particularly poorly. Lethal injection, now the favored method of capital punishment in America, is under scrutiny for being unconstitutional. However, many see the death penalty as a powerful deterrent to crime. Others see the death penalty as a just punishment. Still others argue that capital punishment saves the state the costs associated with long term imprisonment. Should capital punishment be abolished in the United States? Carefully explain the rationale for your position.

Essay 8:
Stem cells can be coaxed to do many different things. But the most versatile stem cells used in research usually come from human embryos. Cloning processes raise ethical dilemmas that are sparking intense political debate. In 2006 George Bush vetoed a bill that would have expanded federal funding for stem-cell research, but other leaders in the field, including China and South Korea, permit cloning for the creation of embryonic stem cells. Should the federal government provide funding for stem-cell cloning research? Carefully explain the rationale for your position.

Essay 9:
Google plans to create a vast digital library including millions of books that would be searchable on line. Google would digitize most books published in the U.S., including those that are out of print. Individuals would be able to search and view small portions of text and would also be able to purchase electronic copies of the books. Google and the copyright holder would share the revenues from these sales. Some argue that making this information more easily available would benefit society as a whole by making obscure books more easily available to the general public. Others argue that this would provide Google with a dangerous monopoly over digital sales of many books, hurting the public with higher prices and the copyright owners by paying them lower royalties. In your opinion, do you believe that Google should be able to freely offer digital versions of books, that this right should be regulated or restricted, or that Google should not be able to offer this service? Carefully explain the rationale for your position.

Essay 10:
British orchestra conductor Sir Edward Downes traveled from the United Kingdom to Switzerland with his wife, who was terminally ill with cancer. At Dignitas, a Swiss assisted suicide clinic, Sir Downes and his wife committed suicide together – even though he was not terminally ill. Some argue that people should be able to choose when to end their lives, and that the government should not prohibit doctors or nurses from providing help with end of life decisions. Others argue that doctors and nurses should only work to prolong or maintain life, rather than to terminate it. Still others believe that suicide or euthanasia should only be allowed for people who are terminally ill. In your opinion, what limits or restrictions, if any, should exist with regards to assisted suicide? Carefully explain the rationale for your position.

Essay 11:
Government support of the visual arts and performing arts is at times controversial. Some argue that there should be no government support of the arts but that market forces and patrons should solely support the arts. Others think some government support should be provided but only under the condition that the art presented is judged acceptable by community standards. Still others, however, argue that the arts play an important role in society and should be supported by government funding without any restrictions or conditions. In your view, what should public policy be in regard to supporting the arts? Carefully explain the rationale for your position.

Essay 12:
Since the closure of the last remaining horse meat slaugtherhouses in 2007, the wild horse population has grown to an estimated 75,000. Each of these horses can drink 5 gallons of water and eat 18 pounds of forage a day, placing a strain on the environment and leaving many hillsides and valleys denuded by overgrazing.

Some people believe that the over population of wild horses can be controlled by shooting some animals or by allowing the reopening of horse slaughterhouses. Other people believe that a better solution would be to neuter horses. A third view is that horses should be moved to habitats where they can live freely or adopted as domestic horses. In your view, how should the wild horse population be managed? Carefully explain the rationale for your position.

Essay 13:
The drone attack policy has resulted in more than 400 attacks in four years, making them the weapon of choice in the fight against terrorism during President Obama's first term. Some argue that this policy is successful because it has decimated the top eschelons of Al Qaeda commanders. Others argue that the drone policy is a failure because it results in the death of thousands of civilians. Still others believe that while successful in targeting Al Qaeda operatives, the drone attacks result in local anger and resentments that ultimately creates the next generation of terrorists. In your view, should the U.S. continue its drone attack policy? Carefully explain the rationale for your position.

Recommended Links

Guide to the Foreign Service Officer Selection Process – pdf file link at bottom of page
http://careers.state.gov/officer/employment.html

Career Track Test
http://careers.state.gov/officer/which-career-track

FSOT test registration
www.act.org/fsot/

FSOT Official Study Guide
www.act.org/fsot/store/index.html

FSOA Official Study Guide (2013 version)
http://careers.state.gov/uploads/ba/ca/bacaddbd75ea89208fa80665d64506cb/FSO_OA_StudyGuide_2013.pdf

FSOA Official Study Guide (Older version)
http://careers.state.gov/uploads/98/f1/98f1f0f4472a93e23bf94b0bde259167/3-0-0_FSO_ORalAssessment_April2012.pdf

Economist Weekly Quiz
http://www.economist.com/economist-quiz

Economist Debates
http://www.economist.com/debate/archive

Christian Science Monitor FSOT Practice Test
http://www.csmonitor.com/USA/Foreign-Policy/2011/0127/Are-you-smarter-than-a-US-diplomat-Take-our-Foreign-Service-Exam/US-History

CIA Factbook
https://www.cia.gov/library/publications/the-world-factbook/index.html

eDiplomat Post Reports
www.ediplomat.com/np/post_reports /post_reports.htm

Acronym	Meaning
AAMOF	As a matter of fact
AAMOI	As a matter of interest
AAR	At any rate
ACK	Acknowledgement
AEAP	As early as possible
AFAIC	As far as I'm concerned
AFAICS	As far as I can see
AFAICT	As far as I can tell
AFAIK	As far as I know
AFAIR	As far as I remember
AFAIU	As far as I understand
AFIAA	As far as I am aware
AFPOE	A fresh pair of eyes
AIMB	As I mentioned before
ASAMOF	As a matter of fact
ASAP	As soon as possible
ATSL	Along the same line
BOTEC	Back of the envelope calculation
FAQ	Frequently asked questions
FWIW	For what it's worth
FYI	For your information
GRAS	Generally recognized as safe
IINM	If I am not mistaken
IIRC	If I remember correctly
IMCO	In my considered opinion
IMHO	In my humble opinion; In my honest opinion
IMO	In my opinion
IMPOV	In my point of view

Acronym	Meaning
ITFA	In the final analysis
IYO	In your opinion
KUTGW	Keep up the good work
LFTI	Looking forward to it
MITIN	More information than I needed
MSTM	Makes sense to me
MTF	More to follow
NBIF	No basis in fact
NIH	Not invented here
NNR	Need not respond
NRN	No reply necessary
OAUS	On an unrelated subject
P&CP	Private & Confidential
POTUS	President of the United States
POV	Point of view
RNN	Reply not necessary
RSVP	Repondez s'il Vous Plait (please respond)
SOP	Standard operating procedure
TWIMC	To whom it may concern
TIA	Thanks in advance
UPOD	Under promise over deliver
URW	You are welcome
WRT	With regard to; With respect to

Made in the USA
Middletown, DE
17 January 2018